HYDROGEOLOGY OF THE MUIR BEACH COMMUNITY

SERVICES DISTRICT WELL SITE, FRANK VALLEY,

REDWOOD CREEK, CALIFORNIA

GOLDEN GATE NATIONAL RECREATION AREA

Larry Martin

Technical Report NPS/NRWRD/NRTR-2000/265

April 2000

United States Department of the Interior

National Park Service

Water Resources Division

Fort Collins, CO

Table of Contents

List of Tables and Figures

Acknowledgements

The potential impact of groundwater pumping on streamflow in Redwood Creek has been an issue with the National Park Service for about 15 years. My involvement in the issue goes back only about one year, and was essentially limited to conducting an aquifer test at the site in July 1999 and compilation and analysis of hydrogeologic information collected by many investigators over the previous years. I hope the information presented in this report will be useful in resolving this issue.

Many persons associated with the National Park Service and Muir Beach Community Services District provided assistance with conducting the aquifer test and in reviewing drafts of this report. Tamara Williams at Golden Gate National Recreation Area provided coordination between NPS and MBCSD in planning and conducting the aquifer test. Tamara also provided much assistance throughout the aquifer test, analysis of test results, and review and discussion of the numerous drafts of this report. Eric Moser with the NPS Water Resources Division assisted with monitoring during the aquifer test and supplied the technical wizardry to keep the dataloggers operating during the test. Bill Van Liew with the NPS Water Resources Division assisted with monitoring, data analysis, and interpretation of test results. Bill Hansen and Dan McGlothlin with the NPS Water Resources Division contributed to review of this work and application of the results to policy issues.

MBCSD provided access to their site and allowed us to monitor water table response at a number of their wells. MBCSD also adjusted their normal pumping operations to facilitate the aquifer testing described in this report. We could not have completed this work without their cooperation.

Abstract

A study was conducted to determine whether pumping groundwater from the Muir Beach Community Services District Supply Well would cause depletion of streamflow in Redwood Creek. It was determined that the alluvial aquifer in Frank Valley is a heterogeneous aquifer that is hydrologically interconnected with surface flow in Redwood Creek. Pumping water from the Muir Beach Community Services District Supply Well induces infiltration from Redwood Creek to the alluvial aquifer. Streamflow depletion was estimated to be 70-80% of the pumping rate of the well.

Impacts of groundwater pumping on streamflow can be minimized by restricting pumping to nighttime hours when streamflow is not being further depleted by evapotranspiration. Water conservation measures by the Muir Beach community will reduce the water demand, lessening the impact of groundwater pumping. Relocating the supply well to a location further downstream would transfer the impact of streamflow depletion about 3000 feet downstream.

Keywords: hydrogeology, Redwood Creek, Muir Beach, water supply, groundwater, streamflow depletion, Golden Gate National Recreation Area

Introduction

Muir Beach is a small community located on the coastal headlands at the mouth of Redwood Creek in southern Marin County. The Muir Beach Community Services District (MBCSD) owns and operates a water distribution system that provides potable water to the community. The water supply source is a shallow well along Redwood Creek on MBCSD property in Frank Valley, approximately 1 mile upstream from the ocean (Figure 1). The MBCSD property is 0.60 acres, including land on both sides of Redwood Creek. The property is surrounded by California State Park and National Park Service lands.

This study was conducted to help determine whether pumping groundwater from the MBCSD Supply Well would cause depletion of streamflow in Redwood Creek. Streamflow depletion could be especially problematic during drought or normal low-flow conditions. Redwood Creek supports native populations of steelhead trout and coho salmon. Reducing streamflow below normal low-flow conditions may cause fish mortality or other impacts to aquatic habitat.

The purposes of this report are to: 1) present the results of aquifer testing conducted at the MBCSD Well Site in July 1999, 2) discuss hydrologic impacts from pumping groundwater at the MBCSD Well Site, and 3) make recommendations to minimize the potential impact of pumping groundwater from the alluvial aquifer on streamflow.

Background

Muir Beach Community Services District (MBCSD) provides potable water to the community of Muir Beach. MBCSD provides water to 147 service connections, supplying approximately 350 persons. MBCSD was formed in 1950 to operate the Bello Subdivision well and water system. The original well supplying the system was near the present location of the Pelican Inn Restaurant and was drilled sometime in 1898 or 1899. That well has been sealed and abandoned. MBCSD acquired the current Well Site on Redwood Creek through its purchase of the Seacape Water Company in 1970. The first

1

well on the current site was drilled prior to 1963. It was located beneath the existing well house, east of the creek. A replacement well was drilled in 1966 or 1967, west of the creek. Additional backup or replacement wells were drilled in 1970, 1982, and 1996. The 1996 well is the current production well and the 1982 well is the current backup well. The other wells were properly sealed and abandoned. (Personal communication, Donovan Macfarlane, General Manager, MBCSD, 2000)

In August 1988, the California State Water Resources Control Board (SWRCB) advised MBCSD that a hydrogeologic investigation of Redwood Creek had determined that the District was diverting underflow water from the creek. MBCSD was requested to submit an application for a water right permit for diversion of surface water. The District claimed that it was legally pumping groundwater and therefore did not need a water right permit. However, in August 1988 in compliance with the SWRCB request, the District filed an application to appropriate water from the defined underflow of Redwood Creek. The application was for 0.07 cfs (45,000 gallons per day).

The National Park Service (National Park Service, 1989) filed two protests to MBCSD's application to appropriate water. One protest was based on "injury to vested rights", citing the need to protect National Park Service (NPS) riparian rights on Redwood Creek downstream of the MBCSD Well Site. The other protest was based on "environmental considerations, public interest, public trust, or other items". The protest states that;

> "The Redwood Creek stream system has been stressed by stream
> alterations near the mouth and by stream diversions along its course,
> resulting in a decline in historic levels of salmon and steelhead resources...
> Water quality degradation in Redwood Creek is suspected to have
> occurred and may be a contributing factor to the decline of salmon and
> steelhead. The NPS is concerned that diversion of water, as described in
> Application 29331, may further contribute to the cumulative impacts to
> water and water-related resources. If this is the case, the diversion as
> described in Application 29331, may not be in the best public interest..."

Groundwater withdrawal for public water supply at the Muir Beach community is only one of the factors potentially affecting environmental values of Redwood Creek. Other factors that may affect environmental values are channel alterations and diversions from the creek. Channel alterations include a dike that prevents surface flow in Green Gulch from entering Redwood Creek, channelization, and construction of a parking lot in the area known as Big Lagoon (Johns, 1993). Redwood Creek has been channelized adjacent to the Banducci flower farm. Tributaries from the west side of the farm have been diverted around the farm fields, preventing them from following their natural course to Redwood Creek. Streamflow diversions occur from Green Gulch at the Zen Center and from springs in the headwaters of Redwood Creek (Johns, 1993). Shallow irrigation wells at the Banducci flower farm are no longer used. When these wells were being used, a large percentage of the water being pumped from the wells was from infiltration of streamflow.

Geographic & Geologic Setting

Redwood Creek is a coastal stream in Marin County, approximately 4 miles long, draining an area of 7½ square miles. The creek originates from springs on Mt. Tamalpais and flows generally south, discharging to the Pacific Ocean through an intermittent tidal lagoon at Muir Beach. The upper part of the creek flows through Redwood Canyon in Muir Woods National Monument. The canyon is steep-sided with a narrow valley floor. Below Muir Woods, the creek flows through Frank Valley for approximately 2 miles before reaching the ocean. Frank Valley has a fairly flat valley floor, ranging from about 200 feet wide at the head of the valley to about 500 feet wide at the lower end of the valley. A schematic geologic cross section through the MBCSD Well Site is shown in Figure 2. Vegetation in the drainage basin is composed of mixed conifer forests in the upper valleys, mixed hardwoods, chaparral, and grasslands on the slopes, and a corridor of riparian vegetation (willows and alders) along Redwood Creek.

Bedrock in the area is comprised of rocks of the Franciscan Group, a series of sedimentary, metamorphic, and igneous rocks of Late Jurassic and Cretaceous age (Jennings, 1977). Redwood Creek has downcut through these rocks forming Redwood

3

Canyon and Frank Valley. Frank Valley has subsequently been partially filled with unconsolidated alluvial deposits. Alluvial fill is common in California coastal valleys and can be several hundred feet thick. These alluvial fills occurred following the rise in sea level at the end of the last glacial age that consequently raised the base level of coastal streams. In response to sea level rise, the streams ceased downcutting and deposited alluvium, building up the valley floors to present elevations. Thickness of alluvium at the MBCSD Well Site is not known. Drillers' reports from construction of the water supply wells indicate the alluvium is at least 37 feet thick (Table 1).

The alluvium is unconsolidated and heterogeneous. Sediment exposed in the stream bank and streambed is a mixture of silt, fine to coarse-grained sand, and pebble–sized gravel. Drillers' logs for wells at the site indicate a variety of sediments were encountered, from clay to gravel. Six deep (35-37 feet) wells have been drilled at the site. Drillers' logs are available for five of the wells (Table 1 and Figure 3). The drillers' logs for these wells are similar, showing heterogeneous layers of clay, sand, and gravel. There is too much heterogeneity and lateral discontinuity to allow correlation of stratigraphic units between wells. While there is some similarity in the stratigraphy at all of the wells, there is enough variability to indicate that the alluvial aquifer should not be described as a multi-layered system of aquifers and aquicludes. Instead, the alluvium is better described as a heterogeneous mix of clay, sand, and gravel, typical of material weathered from Franciscan Formation bedrock and reworked by the flowing water of Redwood Creek.

Drillers' logs for the five deep wells at the MBCSD Well Site are summarized in Table 1 and shown graphically on Figure 3. The drillers' logs indicate what appears to be a heterogeneous aquifer system in which aquifer units and aquitards can not be correlated across the short distances between wells. Most of the intervals containing clay are also described as containing sand or gravel. Thus, it seems reasonable to expect groundwater to be able to move freely throughout the alluvial aquifer system.

Data obtained from hydrologic monitoring at the site supports the conceptual model of a heterogeneous alluvial aquifer system. Monitoring has shown that the water table throughout the area responds to pumping from the MBCSD Supply Well. Monitor wells both close to and distant from the pumped well respond to pumping. Shallow and deep wells respond to pumping. Even shallow wells located within a few feet of the creek show the effects of pumping from the MBCSD Supply Well. Data showing the interconnection of groundwater at all depths in the alluvial aquifer system and at all distances from the creek and well will be presented later in this report.

Site Description

The MBCSD Well Site is approximately 0.60 acres located in Frank Valley, approximately ½ mile upstream from the Shoreline Highway (Hwy 1) bridge. The site includes land on both sides of Redwood Creek and is surrounded by National Park Service and California State Park lands. MBCSD uses the area as a storage and maintenance yard. In addition to being the location of water supply wells, the area is used as a community park by the residents of Muir Beach.

The site is a fairly flat area on the floodplain of Redwood Creek. The channel of Redwood Creek is about 25 feet wide and downcut about 6-8 feet below the valley floor. In addition to supply and monitor wells, the site contains buildings for water treatment and general maintenance by MBCSD, a volleyball court, and various booths and facilities used by the community of Muir Beach for picnics and social gatherings.

Figure 4 is a photograph of the MBCSD Well Site and the lower part of Frank Valley. The MBCSD Well Site is in the lower left of the photo, between the horse riding arena and the road. The large field in the center of the photo is the former Banducci flower farm, downstream of the MBCSD Well Site. A map of the Well Site, showing physical features and property boundaries is shown in Figure 5.

Monitor Wells and Stream Gages

MBCSD has two deep wells (30-35 feet) at the site. Only the new well (constructed in 1996) is currently being used. It will be referred to as the "MBCSD Supply Well" in this report. The older (constructed in 1982) deep well at the site is 10 feet from the MBCSD

Supply Well and is maintained for monitoring purposes and as an emergency backup well. It will be referred to as the "MBCSD Backup Well" throughout this report. MBCSD had drilled another well in 1982 (Well #4), but it was immediately filled and abandoned due to low yield. An older well at the site (Well #3), drilled in 1970, has been filled and abandoned. MBCSD constructed 16 shallow monitor wells in an "X" pattern around the new supply well. These monitor wells are 8-9 feet deep and located approximately 5, 10, 15, and 20 feet from the supply well. They were constructed to monitor the response of the water table in the upper part of the alluvial aquifer (8-9 feet below ground surface) to pumping from wells completed in the lower part of the aquifer (30-35 feet below ground surface). If the MBCSD Supply Well was completed in a confined or semi-confined aquifer, then the water table drawdown in the shallow monitor wells would be less than in the deep monitor wells and it would take longer to occur.

The National Park Service has five shallow piezometers (P-2, P-6, P-8, P-9, and P-10) along the bank of Redwood Creek at the site. These piezometers were constructed by driving 2-foot long drive points (with attached pipe) to various depths, generally 2-4 feet below ground surface. NPS also constructed a deep (35 feet) monitor well near the creek prior to the July 1999 aquifer testing. This well is referred to as the "NPS Monitor Well" throughout this report.

There is one other monitor well at the site; a deep (30 feet) abandoned well located on California State Park land. The well is about 60 feet northwest of the MBCSD Supply Well. Well construction and stratigraphy at this well are not known. This well is referred to as the "State Park Well" throughout this report.

Water level in Redwood Creek was monitored at staff gages attached to piezometers P-8 and P-6. Temporary v-notch weirs were installed in Redwood Creek upstream and downstream of the Well Site.

Table 2 summarizes the depth and perforated intervals for piezometers and monitor wells at the site. Locations of monitor wells, piezometers, staff gages, and weirs are shown on Figure 6.

July 1999 Aquifer Test

An aquifer test was conducted at the MBCSD Well Site in July 1999. The MBCSD Supply Well was used as the pumping well. Water levels in all deep wells and piezometers were monitored throughout the test period. Streamflow in Redwood Creek was monitored upstream and downstream from the MBCSD Well Site. The MBCSD Supply Well had been pumping continuously for several days over the Fourth of July weekend to fill the MBCSD storage tanks. The pump was shut off on the evening of July 7. Water table recovery was monitored for 36 hours. The well was then pumped for 48 hours, followed by an 8-hour recovery period. Average pumping rate during the test was 33 gallons per minute (gpm). Pumping and recovery periods are shown on Figure 7. All water pumped during the test was sent to the MBCSD storage tanks.

Deep Wells

Water levels were monitored in 3 deep wells during the test; the MBCSD Backup Well, an abandoned well on California State Park property (State Park Well), and a new monitor well near Redwood Creek (NPS Monitor Well). The MBCSD Backup Well is the former supply well. It is maintained for monitoring purposes and as an emergency backup well. The yield of the well had decreased and MBCSD constructed a new well in 1996. We have no information about the well on California State Park property; other than the total depth is 32 feet. Presumably, it is completed in the "lower aquifer" with construction similar to the other deep wells. NPS constructed a new deep monitor well just prior to the aquifer test. The well is located a few feet from the creek, about 20 feet downstream from the footbridge. This location is quite close to that of a former MBCSD Supply Well that was constructed in 1970 and abandoned and filled in 1996. Locations of deep wells at the MBCSD Well Site are shown on Figure 6.

In a homogeneous, isotropic aquifer (one that is not affected by recharge from a nearby stream or bounded by a relatively impermeable bedrock barrier) we would expect that water table drawdown would decrease as the distance from the pumped well increased. We would also expect that two observation wells located similar distances from the pumped well would have approximately the same amount of drawdown. This is not what we observed at the MBCSD Well Site.

The MBCSD Backup Well is 10 feet from the MBCSD Supply Well. Water level in the MBCSD Backup Well was drawn down about 1½ feet when the MBCSD Supply Well was pumped at 33 gpm for 48 hours (Figure 8). The State Park Well is 60 feet from the pumped well. Water level in the State Park Well was drawn down about 3 feet when the MBCSD Supply Well was pumped at 33 gpm for 48 hours (Figure 9). The NPS Monitor Well is 65 feet from the pumped well. Water level in the NPS Monitor Well was drawn down about ¾ foot when the MBCSD Supply Well was pumped at 33 gpm for 48 hours (Figure 10).

We would expect to see the greatest amount of drawdown in the MBCSD Backup Well and very close to the same amount of drawdown in both the State Park Well and the NPS Monitor Well. These relationships may not occur if the water table response is affected by recharge from a stream or the presence of an impermeable bedrock boundary (valley wall). The greatest amount of drawdown was observed in the State Park Well. This may be due to the nearby presence of impermeable bedrock bounding the alluvial aquifer as a subsurface expression of the valley wall, or that pumping the MBCSD Supply Well intercepts recharge from the creek before it reaches the State Park Well. Drawdown at the MBCSD Backup Well was only half as much as at the State Park Well, although the MBCSD Backup Well is much closer to the pumped well. Recharge from the creek may be maintaining a higher water table between the creek and the MBCSD Supply Well. We would have expected drawdown in the NPS Monitor Well to be similar to that at the State Park Well, as they are approximately the same distance from the pumped well. We observed much less drawdown at the NPS Monitor Well, but cannot say for certain whether that is a result of stream recharge maintaining a higher water table at the NPS

Monitor Well, the effect of an impermeable boundary near the State Park Well, or some combination of these two effects. When considered together, the data from the deep wells indicate that as the drawdown cone expands around the pumped well, it encounters the effects of both recharge from the creek on one side and increased drawdown from the effects of an impermeable boundary (valley wall) on the other side.

On some of the hydrographs (Figures 8 to 10) there is a noticeable lowering of the water table about mid-day. This may be attributable to a surge or temporary increase in the pumping rate from the MBCSD Supply Well. Alternatively, it could be caused by "pumping" of groundwater by riparian vegetation during the warm sunny part of the day when evapotranspiration is greatest. It may have been caused by a combination of both of these factors. We did not observe this effect at all wells, or on all days. It is most noticeable at mid-day on July 10 at the State Park Well and at mid-day on July 8, 10, and 11at the MBCSD Backup Well.

The elevations of water levels open to the atmosphere, such as water levels in the creek and monitor wells completed in the alluvium, represent the elevation of total hydraulic head. Water always flows from areas of higher hydraulic head to areas of lower hydraulic head. More simply, water flows downhill.

Figure 11 shows a hydrograph of water levels at the three deep monitor wells. The hydrograph shows that during non-pumping periods, water levels at the MBCSD Backup Well and NPS Monitor Well are approximately the same and the water level at the State Park Well is approximately 0.75 feet higher. Water level in the creek was about 0.3 feet lower than the water table elevation at the MBCSD Backup Well or the NPS Monitor Well. Under these conditions, groundwater flow is toward the creek.

During pumping periods, the water level in the creek is the highest, the water level in the NPS Monitor Well is lower than the creek, and the water level in the MBCSD Backup Well is at a lower elevation than either the creek or the NPS Monitor Well. During pumping, the measured water level in the creek remained at the same level,

9

approximately 16.5 feet msl (mean sea level). This is about ½ foot higher than the water level in the NPS Monitor Well, about 1 foot higher than the water level in the MBCSD Backup Well, and about 2 feet higher than the water level in the State Park Well. Under these conditions groundwater flow directions are reversed, with groundwater from the vicinity of the creek flowing toward the pumping well. Also, the water level at the State Park Well is much lower than at the MBCSD Backup Well located 10 feet from the pumping well, possibly showing the effect of an impermeable bedrock valley.

Figure 12 shows a cross section through the site with static and pumping water levels measured in the deep wells. This figure shows that when the MBCSD Supply Well is not being pumped, groundwater flow is toward the creek. When the well is pumped, groundwater flow is from the creek toward the well.

The water level in Redwood Creek adjacent to the NPS Monitor Well remained at 16.5 feet msl throughout the test period, fluctuating only about 0.01foot. Static water level at the NPS Monitor Well was 16.79 feet msl. During pumping, the water level in the NPS Monitor Well was 15.99 feet msl. These data clearly show that the hydraulic gradient (and thus groundwater flow) was toward the creek when the MBCSD Supply Well was not being pumped. When the MBCSD Supply Well was being pumped, the hydraulic gradient (and thus groundwater flow) was from the creek to the alluvial aquifer.

Water level data from the deep wells were analyzed by the Hantush-Jacob method for leaky confined aquifers as described in Lohman (1972). Data were plotted on logarithmic paper and matched to the type curves on Plate 3 (Lohman, 1972) as shown on Figures 13 to 15. These figures show both the matches to the Hantush-Jacob type curves and the departure from the Theis curve. Drawdown data from all three wells shows a departure from the Theis type curves about 100-200 minutes after pumping was started. Measured drawdown after this time was less than would have been expected for a hydrologic system where all of the water was derived from storage in the aquifer. This departure from the Theis curve indicates that there was an additional source of water, other than just aquifer storage, providing water to the well. That additional source of water is almost certainly induced infiltration (recharge) from Redwood Creek.

Analysis of the effects of recharge from the creek is complicated by the distance from the pumped well to the stream and the heterogeneity of the aquifer. For example, the distance from the State Park Well to Redwood Creek is nearly the same in a northeasterly direction as in a southeasterly direction. The presence of discontinuous gravel layers in the alluvial aquifer may provide a direct connection between the creek and some of the monitor wells but not for other monitor wells. It may be that gravelly layers in the upper part of the aquifer provide a pathway for water from the creek to recharge the upper part of the aquifer and then percolate through silt and sandy clay intervals to recharge the lower part of the aquifer. This might account for the small amount of drawdown observed in some of the shallow monitor wells. This vertical leakage of water from an upper zone to a lower zone in the alluvial aquifer could also explain why the rate of drawdown in all of the deep monitor wells decreases at approximately the same time after pumping started.

Data plots for the State Park Well and the MBCSD Monitor Well both show a short period when drawdown was greater than expected (data points above the type curve). This occurs about 7 to 40 minutes after pumping started at the MBCSD Monitor Well and about 25 to 200 minutes after pumping started at the State Park Well. These phenomena may be an effect of an impermeable boundary, such as the buried bedrock forming the boundary of the alluvial aquifer. The time difference for observing this increased drawdown at the two wells may be partly explained by their distance from the creek (the assumed recharge source) or by their distance from the pumped well. The MBCSD Monitor Well is closer to the creek and would exhibit the effects of recharge sooner than the more distant State Park Well. The increased drawdown could be caused by a surge or temporary increase in the pumping rate of the MBCSD Supply Well. An alternative explanation is that the additional drawdown is due to increased evapotranspiration of trees and riparian vegetation at the site, which can resemble the effects of groundwater pumping. Similar increases in drawdown are seen on the data plots about 1500-1700

11

minutes into the test, corresponding with increased evapotranspiration at mid-day on the second day of the pumping period.

Calculated values of transmissivity show the heterogeneity of the aquifer system. Transmissivity based on data from the State Park Well is about 400 ft^2/day. This may represent fine-grained sediments at the edge of the valley. Transmissivity based on data from the MBCSD Backup Well is 1700 ft^2/day and from the NPS Monitor Well, 1300 ft^2/day. These higher values probably represent coarse-grained sediments found near the middle of the valley. Sediments deposited in the valley by a flowing stream formed the alluvial aquifer. Fine-grained sediments would tend to be deposited along the valley margins, usually as floodplain deposits. In the middle of the valley, sediments would tend to be reworked by the meandering of the stream and the fine-grained fraction would be washed downstream, leaving mostly coarse-grained sediments. These sedimentary depositional processes would result in lower transmissivity at wells located toward the margins of the valley and higher transmissivity at wells located near the middle of the valley.

Calculated storage coefficients (2.6×10^{-2}, 8.5×10^{-2}, 1.8×10^{-3}) are characteristic of semi-confined or leaky confined aquifer systems. The range of calculated storage coefficients reflects that the methods of analyses do not account for the complexity of the hydrogeologic setting or the futility of assigning a single value to a hydrologic parameter for a heterogeneous aquifer. Unconfined aquifers generally have a storage coefficient of about 0.1-0.3 and confined aquifers generally have a storage coefficient of about 10^{-5} to 10^{-3} (Heath, 1983).

There are no average values for transmissivity, hydraulic conductivity, or storage coefficient for the alluvial aquifer at the MBCSD Well Site. Site specific hydrogeologic conditions vary from one well to another, depending on the grain size, sorting, and depositional environment for sediments in the vicinity of each well. Wells that penetrate a significant thickness of gravel will produce large quantities of water, while wells that do not penetrate sand or gravel layers (for example MBCSD Well #4) will not yield much water.

Hypothesized hydrogeologic conditions at the site, including the effects of a recharge boundary (Redwood Creek) and an impermeable boundary (bedrock), are shown graphically in Figure 16.

Shallow Piezometers

Water levels were monitored in four shallow piezometers (P-2, P-9, P-6, and P-10) located along the creek bank during the aquifer test (Figure 6). These piezometers were constructed by driving sand points to a few feet below ground surface. Construction depths and perforated intervals for these piezometers are provided in Table 2. The shallow piezometers facilitated measurement of drawdown at the water table immediately adjacent to the creek.

Piezometer P-2 is located 40 feet upstream from the footbridge, on the right bank of the creek, and is screened from 14.9-16.9 feet above msl. Water level in the creek adjacent to the piezometer was approximately 16.9 feet above msl during the aquifer test. Water level in piezometer P-2 rose to 16.8 feet during the recovery period and was drawn down to 16.67 feet during the pumping period, a drawdown of 0.13 feet. Drawdown was observed in piezometer P-2 beginning with the first measurement, 1 minute after the pump was turned on. The water level did not change significantly after 4 hours into the test, probably due to establishment of new equilibrium conditions between the creek, piezometer P-2, and the pumped well. Measured water levels at Piezometer P-2 during the aquifer test are shown on Figure 17.

Piezometer P-9 is located on the upstream side of the footbridge, on the right bank of the creek, and is screened from 14.6-16.6 feet above msl. Water level in the creek adjacent to the piezometer was 16.53 feet above msl during the aquifer test. Water level in piezometer P-9 rose to 16.6 feet during the recovery period and was drawn down to 16.48 feet during the pumping period, a drawdown of 0.12 feet. Drawdown was observed in

13

piezometer P-9 beginning with the first measurement, 2 minutes after the pump was turned on. The water level did not change significantly after 4 hours into the test, probably due to establishment of new equilibrium conditions between the creek, piezometer P-9, and the pumped well. Measured water levels at piezometer P-9 during the aquifer test are shown on Figure 18.

Piezometer P-6 is located 30 feet downstream of the footbridge, in the creek but very near the right bank of the creek, and is screened from 11.4-13.4 feet above msl. Water level in the creek adjacent to the piezometer was 16.5 feet above msl during the aquifer test. Water level in piezometer P-6 rose to 16.5 feet during the recovery period and was drawn down to 16.4 feet during the pumping period, a drawdown of 0.1 feet. Drawdown was observed in piezometer P-6 beginning with the first measurement--4 minutes after the pump was turned on. The water level did not change significantly after 2 hours into the test, probably due to establishment of new equilibrium conditions between the creek, piezometer P-6, and the pumped well. Measured water levels at piezometer P-6 during the aquifer test are shown on Figure 19.

Piezometer P-10 is located 30 feet downstream of the footbridge, on the right bank of the creek, and is screened from 13.8-15.8 feet above msl. Water level in the creek adjacent to the piezometer was 16.5 feet above msl during the aquifer test. Water level in piezometer P-6 rose to 16.6 feet during the recovery period, probably in response to water level recovery in the aquifer and raising of the water level in the creek from impounding water behind the weir. The water level in piezometer P-10 did not change significantly in response to pumping or recovery periods of the aquifer test. The water level fluctuated within a few hundredths of a foot of 16.60 feet msl. The lack of change may have been caused by impoundment of water in the creek at a level adjacent to the perforated interval of the piezometer located 1 foot from the creek--essentially creating a constant head condition. Changes of 0.01-0.02 foot may be attributed to measurement error, or slight differences in technique of the individuals making the measurements. Measured water levels at piezometer P-6 during the aquifer test are shown on Figure 20.

Water levels in the shallow piezometers next to the creek were drawn down almost immediately following the start of pumping. This clearly indicates a hydraulic connection between pumping from the MBCSD Supply Well and drawdown in the alluvial aquifer adjacent to Redwood Creek. Water level drawdown in the piezometers quickly stabilized and then remained relatively constant for the duration of the aquifer test. This indicates that recharge from Redwood Creek was maintaining water levels in the alluvial aquifer, acting as a constant head source of recharge.

Shallow Monitor Wells

There are 16 shallow monitor wells constructed by MBCSD in close proximity to the MBCSD Supply Well (Figure 6). These monitor wells are in an "X" pattern, at distances of 5, 10, 15, and 20 feet from the MBCSD Supply Well. The monitor wells were installed by augering down to about 9 feet deep and placing perforated drainpipe in the hole. We followed the naming convention used by MBCSD for these wells and refer to them as 5-E, 10-N, etc. Well 5-E is 5 feet northeast of the MBCSD Supply Well. Well 10-N is 10 feet northwest of the MBCSD Supply Well. Note that wells labeled "E" are northeast, wells labeled "N" are northwest, wells labeled "W" are southwest, and wells labeled "S" are southeast of the MBCSD Supply Well.

The shallow monitor wells provide a measure of drawdown at the water table near the pumped well. Comparison of drawdown at the water table with drawdown in monitor wells completed at the base of the aquifer allows assessment of vertical hydraulic conductivity of the aquifer. If the MBCSD Supply Well pumps water from a lower confined aquifer that is not hydrologically connected with surface flow in Redwood Creek, as some have claimed, then there should be little or no drawdown observed in these shallow monitor wells.

During construction of the shallow monitor wells, a 4-inch PVC cap was placed over one end of a length of PVC drainpipe. The end with the cap was placed in a hole that had been augered to below the water table. The PVC cap was intended to prevent soil from entering through the bottom of the monitor well. This cap also effectively creates a reservoir of water in the bottom of the well below the lowermost hole in the sidewall of the drainpipe. What appears to be a stable water level during the drawdown portion of the aquifer test may be repeated measurements of water trapped in the bottom of the monitor well. We don't know for certain that the water table was only drawn down about a foot during pumping, as would be suggested from looking at the data plots. A preponderance of data from the 16 shallow monitor wells strongly suggests that the water table is drawn down about a foot when the MBCSD Supply Well is pumped. Water levels in the shallow monitor wells quickly reach equilibrium, suggesting that there is good hydraulic communication between the upper and lower parts of the alluvial aquifer. This also suggests that recharge occurs by infiltration from Redwood Creek.

Data from shallow monitor wells located 5 feet and 20 feet in each direction from the pumped well are shown in Figures 21 to 24. These data are representative of the water level changes in the shallow monitor wells near the MBCSD Supply Well.

Water levels in the shallow monitor wells are drawn down 0.8 to 1.1 feet when the MBCSD Supply Well is pumped. Drawdown in the MBCSD Backup Well stabilizes at about 1.4 feet during pumping. Water levels in wells closer to Redwood Creek (5-E, 20-E, 20-S) are drawn down less than wells further from Redwood Creek. This is probably due to the increased effect of recharge from Redwood Creek on wells closer to the creek.

Water level data from the shallow monitoring wells support our conceptual model of induced infiltration from Redwood Creek. As water levels in the alluvial aquifer are lowered, there is increased recharge from Redwood Creek to the aquifer. Recharge would occur primarily upstream and adjacent to the Well Site. This water flows laterally toward the pumped well through discontinuous gravel and sand beds in the upper part of the alluvial aquifer. It then percolates downward through the sand, silty sand, and clay gravel deposits to the basal part of the alluvial aquifer and the perforated interval of the pumped well. The slight difference in drawdown between the MBCSD Backup Well and the adjacent shallow monitor wells (5-S and 20-S) further illustrates the vertical recharge of water from the upper to lower parts of the alluvial aquifer. This difference also indicates that water levels in the upper part of the aquifer are being maintained by recharge from some source (such as Redwood Creek). Otherwise, drawdown in the shallow monitor wells would continue to increase during the course of the aquifer test until water levels in the shallow monitor wells were in equilibrium with water levels in the deep monitor wells.

Streamflow

Two 90° v-notch weirs were installed in Redwood Creek during the aquifer test period in July 1999 (Figure 6). One weir was about 300 feet upstream from the MBCSD Well Site and was fairly effective for monitoring changes in flow during the test period. Water level stage at the upstream v-notch was affected by diurnal fluctuations, ranging from about 0.15 feet above the v-notch to 0.25 feet above the v-notch (Figure 25). Streamflow corresponding to these stages ranges from 0.02 to 0.08 cfs (9 to 36 gpm). The diurnal fluctuation, measured at the upstream weir, is about 0.06 cfs (27 gpm). Diurnal fluctuation occurred regardless of whether the well was being pumped. It appears that the amount of diurnal fluctuation at this location is more dependent on local weather (warm, sunny days vs. cool, cloudy or foggy days) rather than operation of the MBCSD Supply Well.

In the analysis of data from the upstream weir, it was assumed that the amount of underflow through the streambed and adjacent gravel bar was constant throughout the test period. Groundwater flow through the gravel bar and streambed is proportional to the difference in water level between the pool upstream from the weir and the creek downstream from the weir. More leakage (as underflow through the gravel streambed) would occur when the water level in the upstream pool was higher. If we were able to measure all of the water flowing in the creek and underlying gravel, we would have shown a larger diurnal fluctuation.

The second weir was installed about 100 feet downstream of the footbridge. At the downstream weir higher flows during the night overflowed or bypassed the sandbag dam constructed to divert water through the v-notch weir. Flow measurements through the v-notch of the downstream weir were essentially constant throughout the test period. The depth of water flowing through the weir was about 0.45 feet, or 0.34 cfs. It was observed that the amount of water flowing over or around the sandbag dam increased at night when evapotranspiration was minimal. Although diurnal fluctuation of streamflow was observed at the downstream weir site, we were unable to quantify the range of diurnal fluctuation due to the leakiness of the weir installation. We also could not make comparisons between the upstream and dowstream weirs to quantify streamflow losses from induced infiltration during pumping of the MBCSD Supply Well.

Instantaneous streamflow was measured by standard gaging techniques with a pygmy meter at two locations on July 12, following the aquifer test. Streamflow downstream from the footbridge was 0.37 cfs, and flow upstream of the upstream weir was 0.39 cfs.

The stage in Redwood Creek was monitored at staff gages attached to piezometers P-6 (about 30 feet downstream of the foot bridge) and P-8 (on the upstream side of the foot bridge. Water surface elevations at the two sites are shown on Figure 26. The rise at the beginning of the hydrograph (July 7-8) is a result of the creek being impounded behind the downstream weir. Otherwise, the hydrographs show no significant changes in the stage of Redwood Creek during the aquifer testing.

Streamflow in Redwood Creek at the MBCSD Well Site was approximately 0.35-0.40 cfs during the test period. Diurnal fluctuation at the upstream weir was on the order of 0.06 cfs (27 gpm). The MBCSD Supply Well was pumped at a rate of about 33 gpm, or 0.07 cfs. It is likely that we may not be able to measure the effects of groundwater pumping on streamflow in the natural channel of Redwood Creek when the MBCSD Supply Well is pumped at low rates, such as 33 gpm. That doesn't mean that streamflow depletion does not occur, only that streamflow in a natural channel could not be measured accurately enough to detect it. Installation of artificial structures, such as weirs or flumes to control flow in the channel, might provide the accuracy needed to detect streamflow depletion.

Discussion

The alluvium in the Redwood Creek valley constitutes a single aquifer. It is heterogeneous, consisting of many lenticular, discontinuous deposits of sedimentary material deposited by Redwood Creek. Groundwater throughout the valley is hydraulically interconnected. Pumping water from the MBCSD Supply Well causes drawdown in monitor wells and piezometers in all directions from the pumped well and at all depths in the aquifer. Drawdown was observed in shallow wells next to the creek and deep wells and shallow wells next to the pumped well. The amount of drawdown observed in various monitor wells is affected by stratigraphy and local hydrogeologic conditions.

Groundwater in the alluvial aquifer and surface water in Redwood Creek are part of an integrated hydrologic system. The waters are clearly interconnected. Water can not be taken from any source in the valley without affecting other components of the hydrologic system. Pumping groundwater from the MBCSD Supply Well lowers the water table in the general vicinity of the well. Lowering the water table results in either intercepting groundwater that would otherwise have discharged to the creek or inducing infiltration from the creek to the groundwater system. Either scenario results in less water in the creek.

These concepts are discussed in detail by McWhorter and Sunada (1977),

> "A well pumping from an aquifer that is intersected by a stream derives a portion of its discharge from aquifer storage and part from induced flow from the stream. At small time, practically all of the pumped water is derived from storage....At large pumping times, the drawdown caused by pumping induces an increasingly larger inflow from the stream as the radius of influence expands....at large t...the discharge from the stream to the aquifer approaches the well discharge, Q."

These concepts agree with the observed data from the aquifer test. As time (t) increases and more of the pumped water is obtained from induced infiltration of streamflow, the rate of drawdown in the aquifer decreases. The rate of drawdown decreases faster than would be predicted as shown by the departure of the data from the Theis Curve as shown in Figures 13-15. When the plot of drawdown flattens (approaching steady-state conditions), the cone of depression is no longer expanding. This is an indication that the rate of recharge from Redwood Creek to the aquifer has become equilibrated with pumping from the MBCSD Supply Well.

The pumping rate (33 gpm or 0.07 cfs) of the MBCSD Supply Well was too small to produce a measurable change in streamflow in Redwood Creek in this study. That does not mean there was no streamflow depletion but that the ability to measure streamflow (in this study) in natural channels did not have enough precision.

Diurnal fluctuation of flow in Redwood Creek measured during the aquifer test was probably caused by evapotranspiration. The amount of observed diurnal fluctuation was approximately the same as the current pumping rate of the MBCSD Supply Well. So one might ask why we couldn't measure streamflow depletion due to pumping of the well if we could measure diurnal fluctuation. The primary reason is that there was too much leakage at the downstream weir site.

Estimation of Streamflow Depletion by Analytical Methods

Streamflow depletion at the MBCSD Well Site was estimated using the method described by Jenkins (1970). The method makes a number of assumptions regarding the hydrogeologic system to be analyzed. It assumes that the aquifer is homogeneous, isotropic and has a semi-infinite areal extent. It also assumes that a stream forms a straight-line boundary to the aquifer and that the stream fully penetrates the aquifer. Site conditions rarely, if ever, meet these conditions. However, the method can still be used to provide an approximation of streamflow depletion from a nearby pumping well.

At the MBCSD Well Site, the aquifer is not homogeneous, isotropic, and semi-infinite in areal extent. The creek does not form a straight boundary nor does it fully penetrate the aquifer. The heterogeneity of the aquifer and the fact that the creek does not fully penetrate the aquifer may reduce streamflow depletion. Meandering of Redwood Creek results in a longer stream reach being in close proximity to the well, which increases the streamflow depletion since a longer reach of the creek is influenced by the cone of depression surrounding the well. The results of the following analysis provide an approximation of streamflow depletion at Redwood Creek from pumping the MBCSD Supply Well.

The theoretical basis of the Jenkins method is identical to that of Theis and Conover (1963) and Glover and Balmer (1954). Jenkins presents a graphical method for solving the governing equations. The method requires computation of a stream depletion factor, defined as:

$$sdf = \frac{a^2 S}{T}$$

Where:

sdf = stream depletion factor

a = distance from the stream to the pumped well

S = specific yield of the aquifer

T = transmissivity of the aquifer

Using values based on data from the July 1999 aquifer test we get the following results:

a = 70 feet

S = .05

T = 1500 feet^2/day

$$sdf = \frac{(70\,ft)^2\,(.05)}{1500\,ft^2\,/\,day} = 0.163\,day$$

Next the parameter t/sdf is calculated for various pumping times, t. Using the value of t/sdf, q/Q (the percentage of pumped water obtained from depletion of the stream) is determined, where q is the rate of stream depletion and Q is pumping rate of the well.

The value q/Q is obtained graphically from Figure 1 or interpolation from Table 1 in Jenkins (1970). For the MBCSD Supply Well the following results are obtained:

t, days	t/sdf	q/Q
0.5	3.1	.69
1	6.1	.77
2	12.3	.84
3	18.4	.87

These results indicate that when the MBCSD Supply Well is pumped, induced infiltration of streamflow from Redwood Creek occurs at a rate of approximately 70-85% of the pumping rate of the well

Another method to evaluate the potential magnitude of induced infiltration is to treat the problem analogously to a MODFLOW river leakage problem (McDonald and Harbaugh, 1984). In this case, leakage through a reach of a riverbed is approximated by Darcy's Law as:

$$QRIV = \frac{KLW(HRIV - HAQ)}{M}$$

Where:

QRIV is the leakage through the reach of the riverbed (induced infiltration)

K is the hydraulic conductivity of the riverbed

L is the length of the riverbed

W is the width of the riverbed

HAQ is the head (water level) in the aquifer

HRIV is the head (water level) in the river

At the MBCSD Well Site measured values of (HRIV-HAQ) during pumping include: 0.23 foot at piezometer P-2, 0.05 foot at piezometer P-9, and 0.1 foot at piezometer P-6. An

22

average value of 0.1 foot was used for the analyses. The thickness of the riverbed (M) is assumed to be 1 foot. Riverbed thickness is probably irrelevant for this analysis, as the riverbed sediments are simply reworked alluvial material, with the fine-grained portion washed away by streamflow. The average width of the streambed (W) was estimated to be 5 feet. The affected length of the riverbed within the cone of depression of the pumped well (L) is estimated to be 200 feet. This distance was estimated by measuring the distance between piezometers where drawdown was observed (the distance between P-2 and P-6 is about 100 feet) and making further estimates of the reach of the creek likely affected--based on the location of the pumped well, the curvature of the stream meanders, and the distance to the stream from the pumped well. Hydraulic conductivity (K) was estimated to be 100 ft/day, based on data from the aquifer test and professional judgement regarding hydraulic conductivity of stream sediments.

Using the estimated parameters described above, streamflow depletion from pumping the MBCSD Supply Well can be estimated:

$$QRIV = \frac{(100\,ft\,/\,day)(200\,ft)(5\,ft)(0.1\,ft)}{1\,ft}$$

$$QRIV = 10{,}000 \text{ ft}^3/\text{day} = 75{,}000 \text{ gpd} = 50 \text{ gpm}$$

This analysis clearly shows that a large quantity of water, more than is pumped from the MBCSD Supply Well, can infiltrate from Redwood Creek to the alluvial aquifer over a relatively short reach of the creek, with a minimal head differential between the creek and the aquifer.

Conclusions and Recommendations

1. The alluvium in the Redwood Creek valley constitutes a single heterogeneous aquifer.

2. Surface water in Redwood Creek and groundwater in the alluvial aquifer are hydraulically interconnected.

3. Groundwater pumping at the MBCSD Well Site in Frank Valley reduces streamflow by inducing infiltration of surface water to the alluvial aquifer.

4. Streamflow depletion is estimated to be approximately 70-80% of the pumping rate of the well.

Impacts of groundwater pumping at the MBCSD Well Site can be reduced by implementing the following measures:

1. Reduce water use during summer and fall as much as possible. Impacts of groundwater pumping on streamflow are proportionately greater when streamflow is low, generally June through November.

2. Increase storage and pumping capacity so that it isn't necessary to pump during the daytime when streamflow is low and evapotranspiration is high (generally June-November). Pumping during the daytime compounds the impact of evapotranspiration on streamflow.

3. Investigate the possibility of relocating water supply well(s) further downstream. Locating a well near the intersection of Hwy 1 and the Frank Valley Road would move the location of impacts downstream approximately 3000 feet. Streamflow depletion might be reduced by locating the well farther from the creek.

References

Cardwell, G.T., 1958, Geology and Ground Water in the Santa Rosa and Petaluma Valley Areas, Sonoma County, California: U.S. Geological Survey Water Supply Paper 1427, 273 pages

Glover, R.E., and G.G. Balmer, 1954, River Depletion Resulting from Pumping to a Well Near a River, Trans. American Geophysical Union, Vol. 35, pp 468-470

Harding-Lawson and Associates, 1991, Water Supply Evaluation, Letter Report to Muir Beach Community Services District

Heath, Ralph C., 1983, Basic Ground-Water Hydrology, U.S. Geological Survey Water-Supply Paper 2220, 85 pages

Jenkins, C.T., 1970, Computation of Rate and Volume of Stream Depletion by Wells, USGS Techniques of Water-Resources Investigations of the United States Geological Survey, Book 4, Chapter D1, 17 pages

Jennings, C.W., 1977, Geologic Map of California: California Geologic Data Map series, California Division of Mines and Geology

Johns, Alice E., 1993, Redwood Creek Water Rights Assessment, Golden Gate National Recreation Area, National Park Service Technical Report NPS/NRWRD/NRTR-93/16

Ketcham, Brannon J., 1998, Hydrologic Monitoring Station Information Summary, National Park Service, Coho and Steelhead Restoration Project, Point Reyes National Seashore

Laudon, Julie, 1988, Redwood Creek Underflow, Marin County, Memorandum to files, Division of Water Rights, State Water Resources Control Board, 9 pages

Lohman, S.W., 1972, Ground-Water Hydraulics, USGS Professional Paper 708, 70 pages

McDonald, Michael G., and Arlen W. Harbaugh, 1984, A modular Three-Dimensional Finite-Difference Ground-Water Flow Model, USGS Open-File Report 83-875, 528 pp.

McWhorter, David B., and Daniel K. Sunada, 1977, Ground-Water Hydrology and Hydraulics, Water Resources Publications, Fort Collins, Colorado, 290 pp.

National Park Service, 1989, Protest to Application 29331 filed with the State Water Resources Control Board, Division of Water Rights

National Park Service, ----, Hydrologic Study to Resolve Redwood Creek Water Rights Dispute, Project Statement GOGA-N-005.5, Golden Gate National Recreation Area, 16 pages

Peltier, Tom, 1998, Review of Report on Hydrogeology of Muir Beach Community Services District Water Supply Well, Memo to File, California State Water Resources Control Board, 2 pages

Phillip Williams and Associates, Ltd., 1995, Analysis of Land Use Impacts on Water Quality and Quantity in Redwood Creek, 33 pages

Theis, Charles V. and Clyde S. Conover, 1963, Chart for Determination of the Percentage of Pumped Water Being Diverted From a Stream or Drain, in Shortcuts and Special Problems in Aquifer Tests, USGS Water Supply Paper 1545-C, pages C106-C109

Trihey & Associates, Inc., 1997, Letter report to Muir Beach Community Services District RE: Well Production Water Supply Alternatives/Mitigation, 9 pages

TABLES

Table 1. Summary of drillers' logs for wells at MBCSD well site.

NPS Monitor Well, drilled July 1999

Depth from surface, feet	Description
0-4	Brown gravely silt
4-12	Silty sand, gravel and cobbles
12-16	Gray sandy clay
16-21	Brown silty sandy gravel
21-25	Brown sand, some gravel
25-30	Brown sandy gravel, some clay
30-35	Gray sandy silt and clay
35-36½	Yellow brown sandstone, weathered and dense

MBCSD Supply Well, drilled June 1996

Depth from surface, feet	Description
0-1½	Topsoil
1½-11	Brown clay with rock
11-12½	River gravel
12½-32	Grey clay with rock
32-36	Gravel, little binder
36-37	Hard impervious rock

MBCSD Backup Well, drilled July 1982

Depth from surface, feet	Description
0-7	Brown clay with gravel
7-10	Gravel
10-12	Brown clay with gravel
12-15	Blue sand, clay and gravel
15-32	Blue clay and gravel
32-33	Green clay and gravel
33-36	Brown clay with boulders

Table 1. Summary of drillers' logs for wells at MBCSD well site.
cont.

MBCSD Well #3, drilled October 1970, plugged and abandoned July 1996

Depth from surface, feet	Description
0-3	Topsoil
3-8	Brown clay, sand, gravel
8-10	Brown gravel
10-15	Brown sandy clay
15-17	Blue gravel
17-24	Blue sandy clay
24-29	Blue gravel
29-33	Brown and yellow sand and clay
33-36	Brown gravel

MBCSD Well #4, drilled and sealed July 1982

Depth from surface, feet	Description
0-6	Brown clay and sand
6-11	Brown clay and gravel
11-15	Brown clay
15-18	Blue clay, sand and water
18-24	Blue clay
24-31	Blue clay, sand and water
31-34	Blue clay
34-36	Brown clay and boulders

Well Name	Distance From Pumped Well, Feet	Total Depth, Feet	Ground Surface, Elevation MSL	Perforated Interval, Elevation MSL
MBCSD Supply Well	0	36	25.46 (top of casing)	-12 to +4
MBCSD Backup Well	10	Approx. 36	24.47 (top of casing)	Approx. -12 to +4
State Park Well	60	32	25.55	Unknown
NPS Monitor Well	65	34.5	23.14	Approx. -12 to +4
P-2	62	3.75	18.65	14.9 to 16.9
P-9	68	4.3	18.91	14.6 to16.6
P-10	100	4.5	18.36	13.8 to 15.8
P-6	98	3.6	15.05	11.4 to 13.4
MBCSD Piezometers	5 – 20	8 to 9	23.5 to 24.2	Entire depth

Table 2. Construction details for wells at MBCSD Well Site.

FIGURES

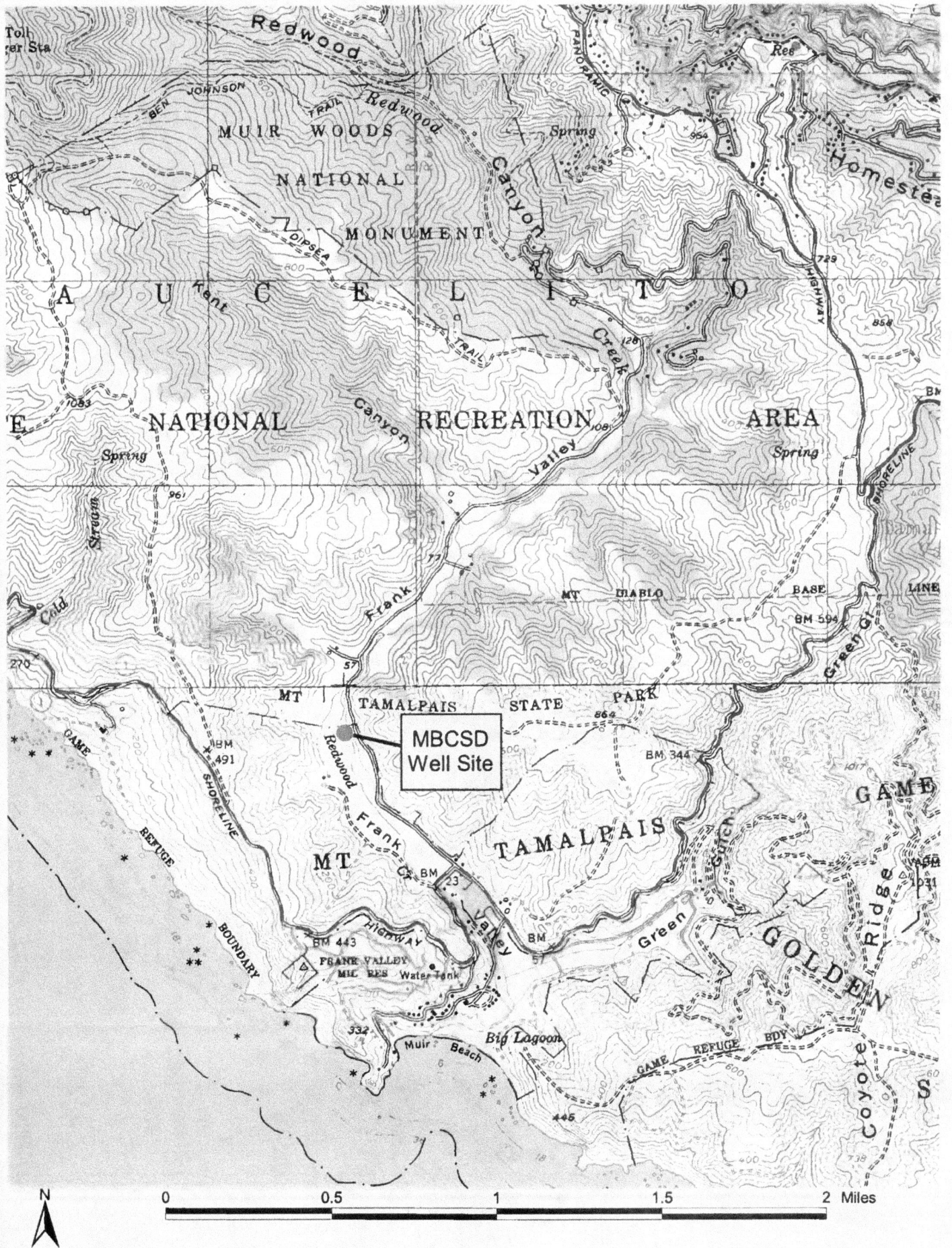

Figure 1. Location of Muir Beach Community Services District Well Site in Frank Valley

Figure 2. Generalized West-East cross section at MBCSD Well Site

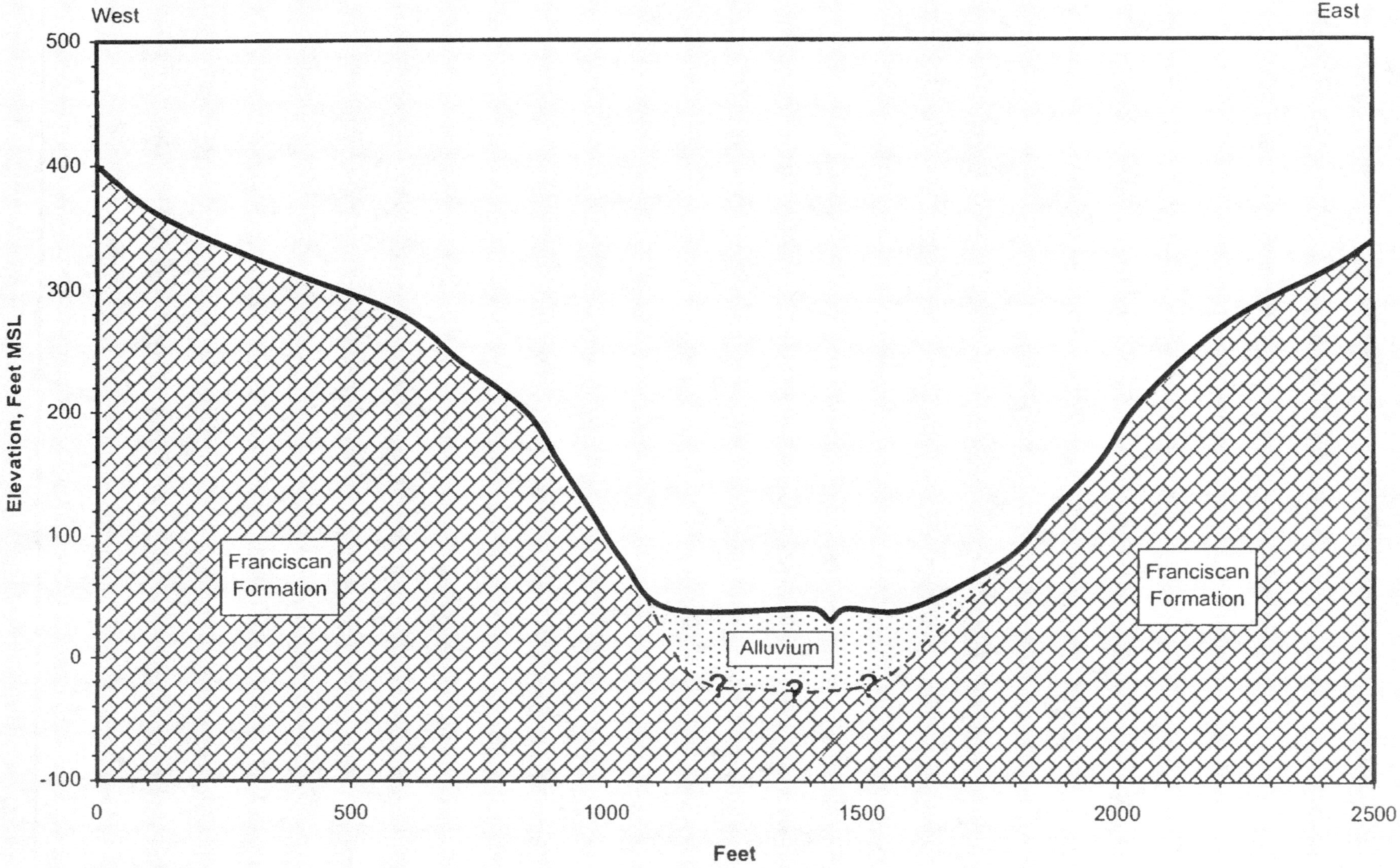

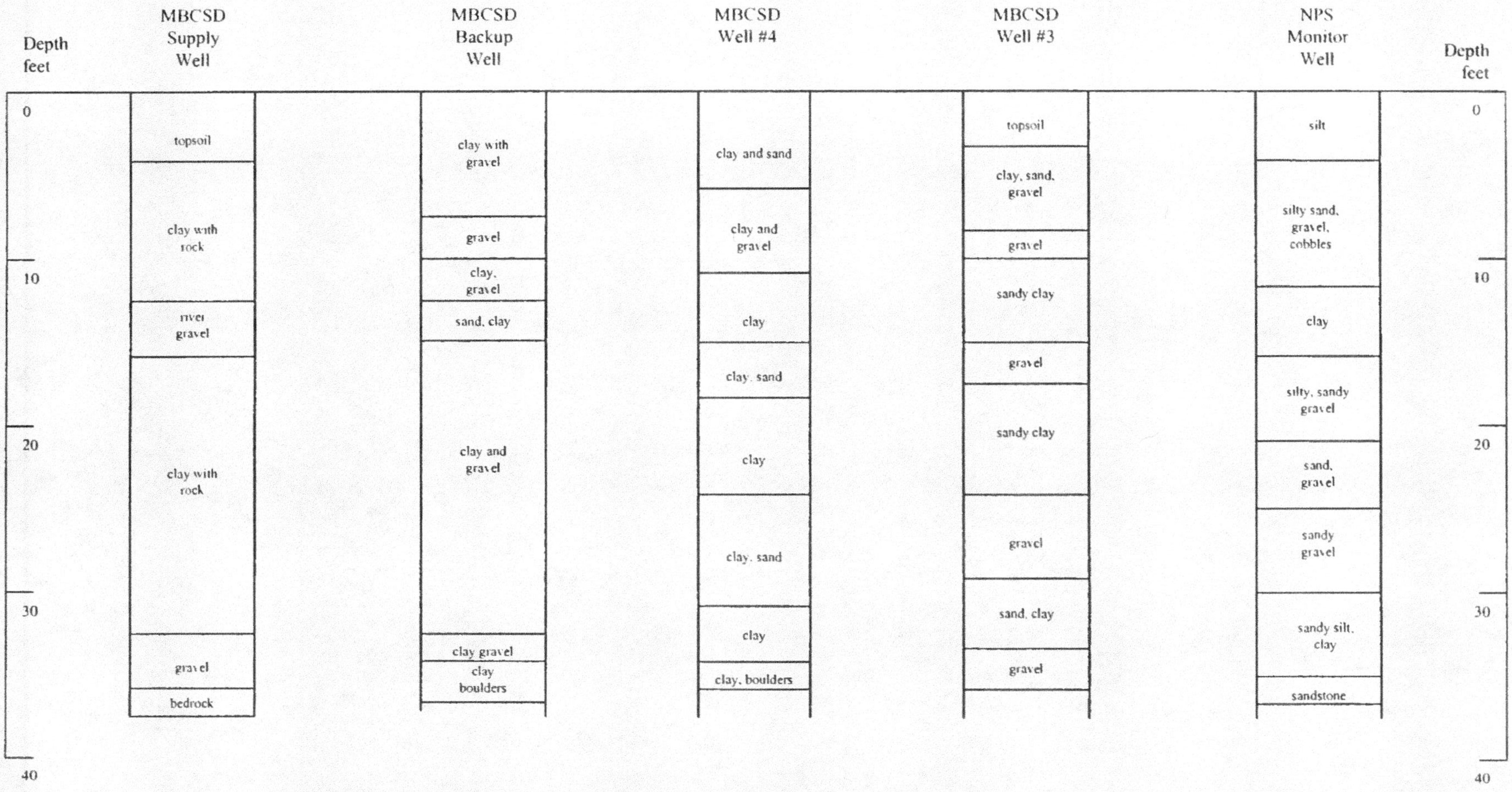

Figure 3. Schematic cross section showing stratigraphy based on drillers' logs

Well Site

Figure 4. Photo of Muir Beach Community Services District well site, July 1999. View is looking down Frank Valley, toward the south.

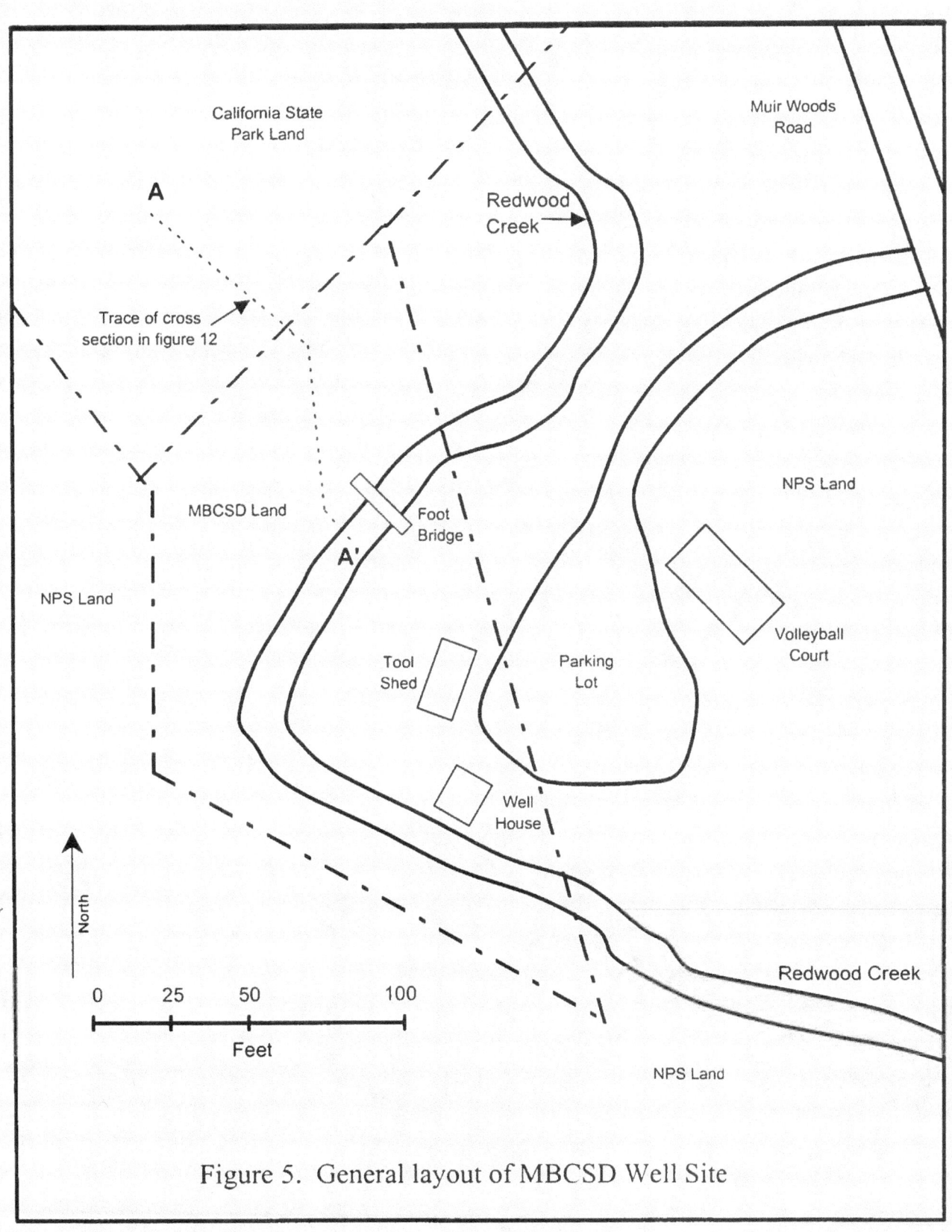

California State
Park Land

A

Trace of cross
section in figure 12

Redwood
Creek

Muir Woods
Road

NPS Land

MBCSD Land

Foot
Bridge

A'

NPS Land

Tool
Shed

Parking
Lot

Volleyball
Court

Well
House

North

0   25   50   100

Feet

Redwood Creek

NPS Land

Figure 5. General layout of MBCSD Well Site

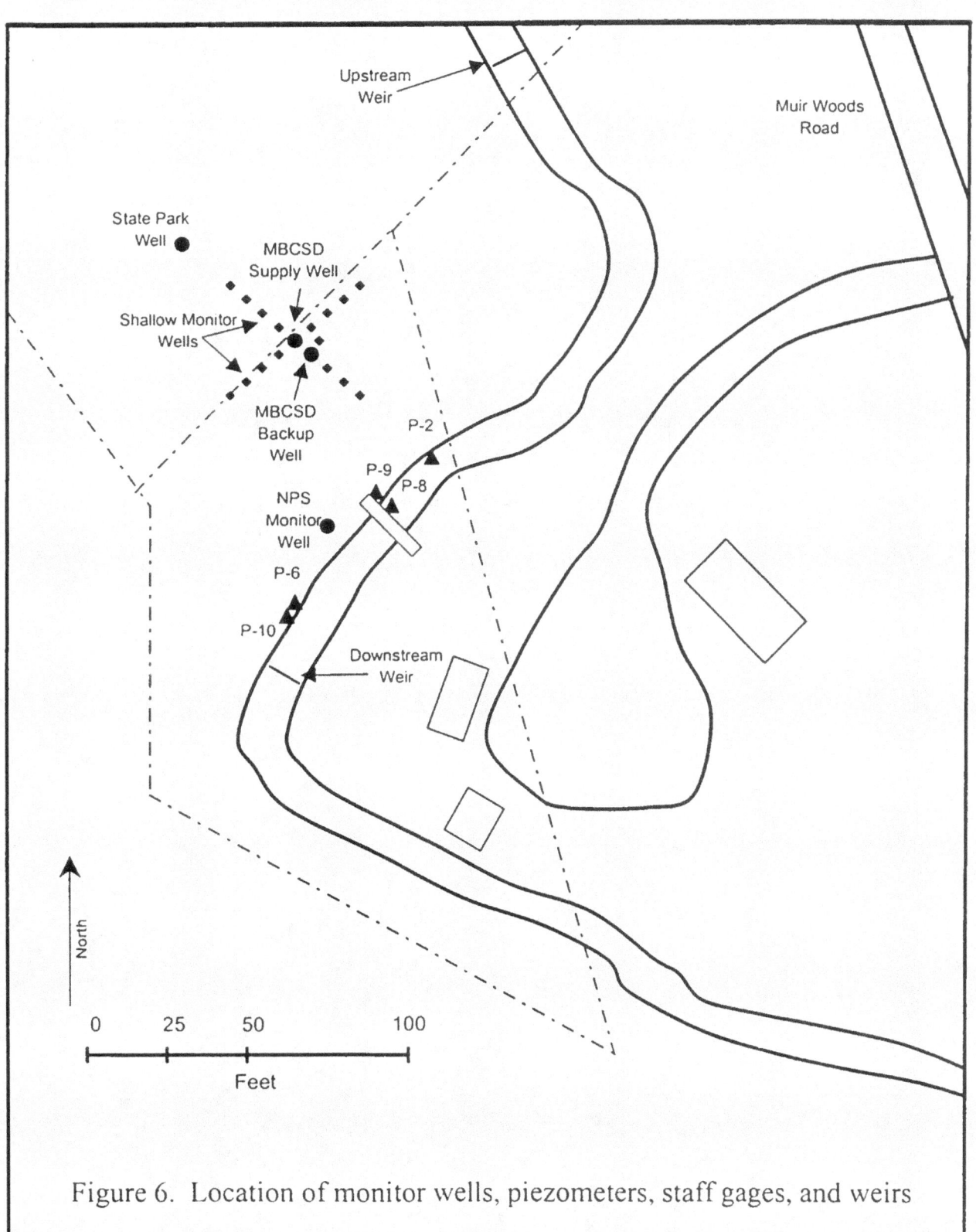

Figure 6. Location of monitor wells, piezometers, staff gages, and weirs

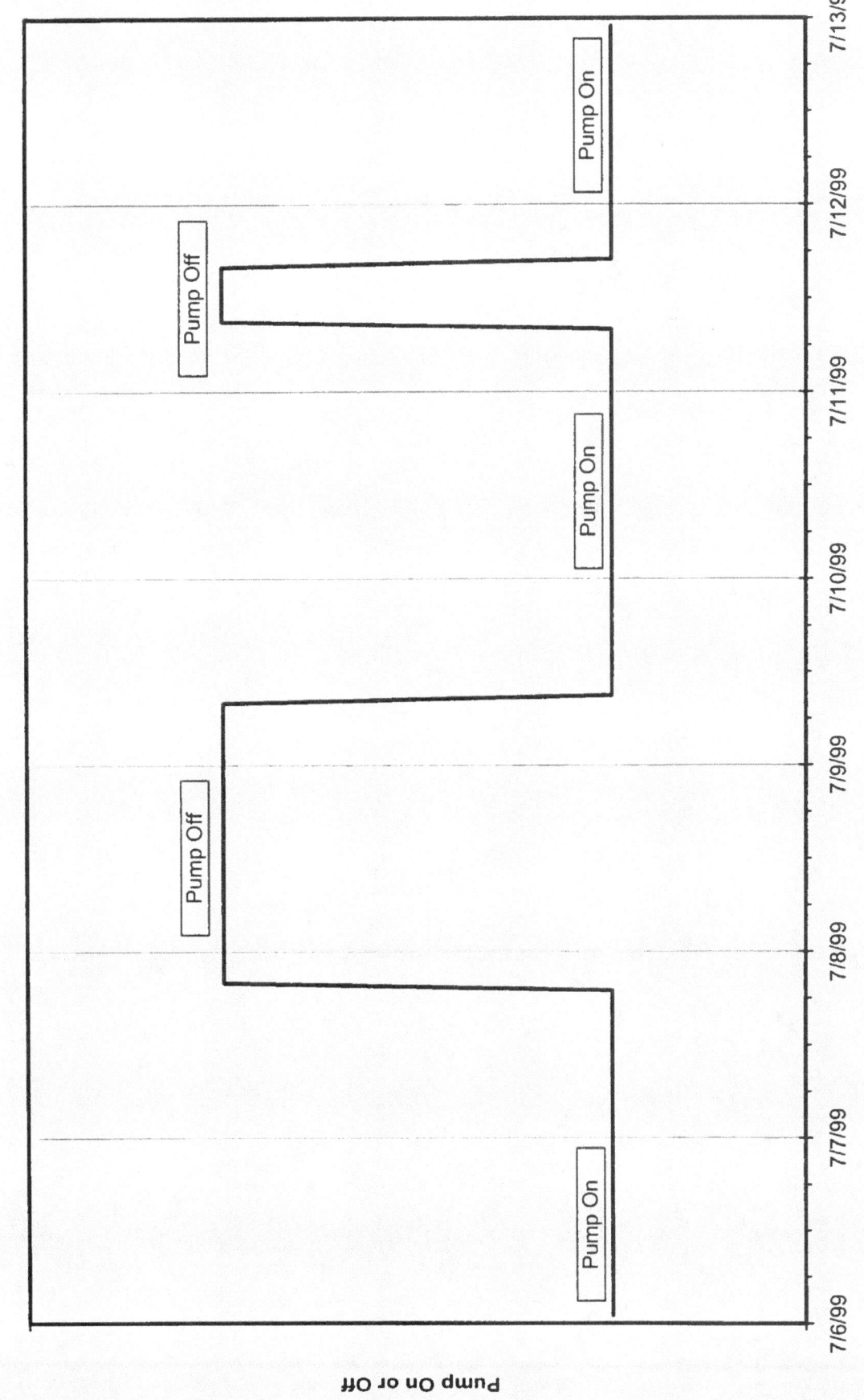

Figure 7. Pumping and recovery periods for the July 1999 aquifer test at the MBCSD Well Site

Figure 8. Hydrograph of MBCSD Backup Well during the July 1999 aquifer test

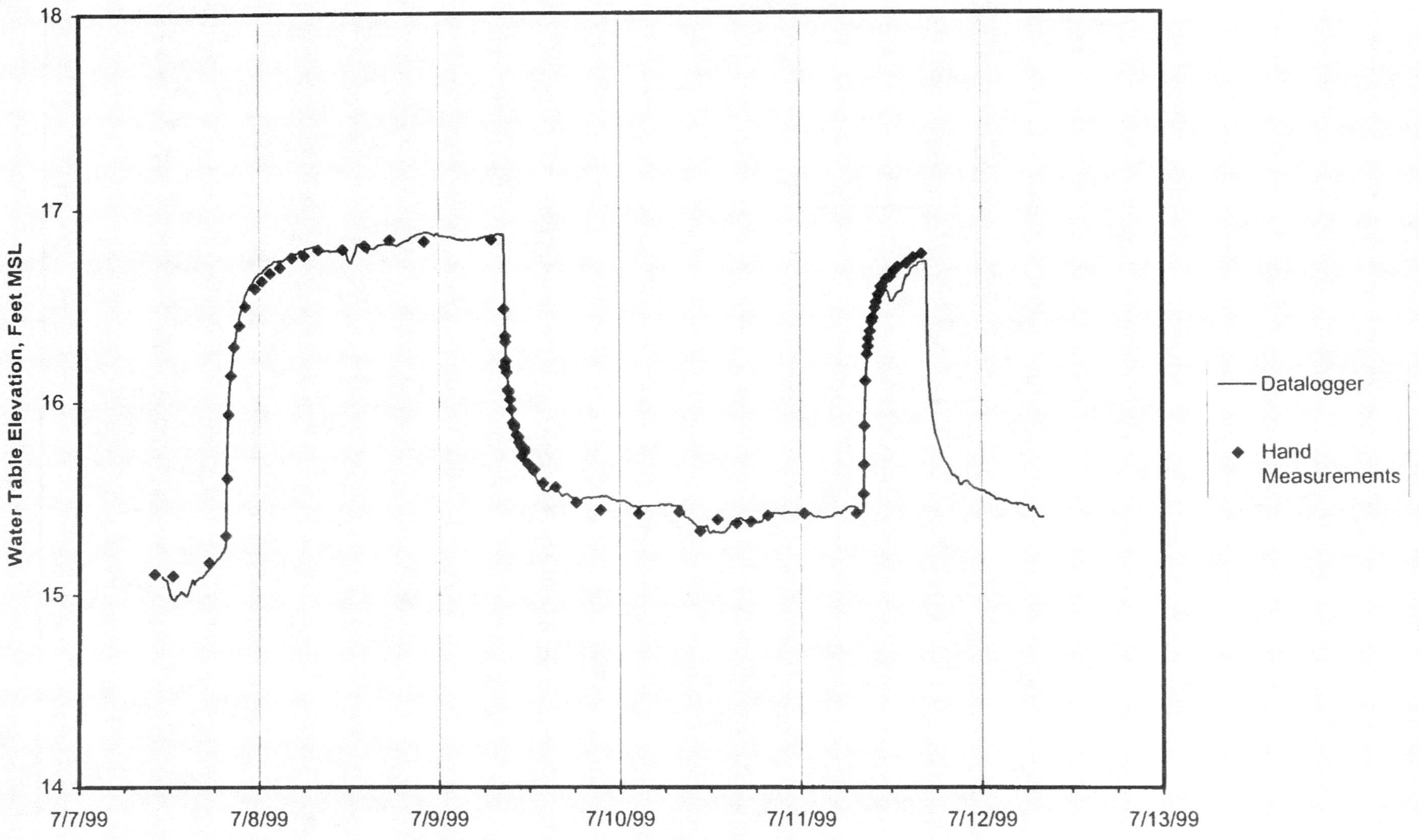

Figure 9. Hydrograph of State Park Well during the July 1999 aquifer test

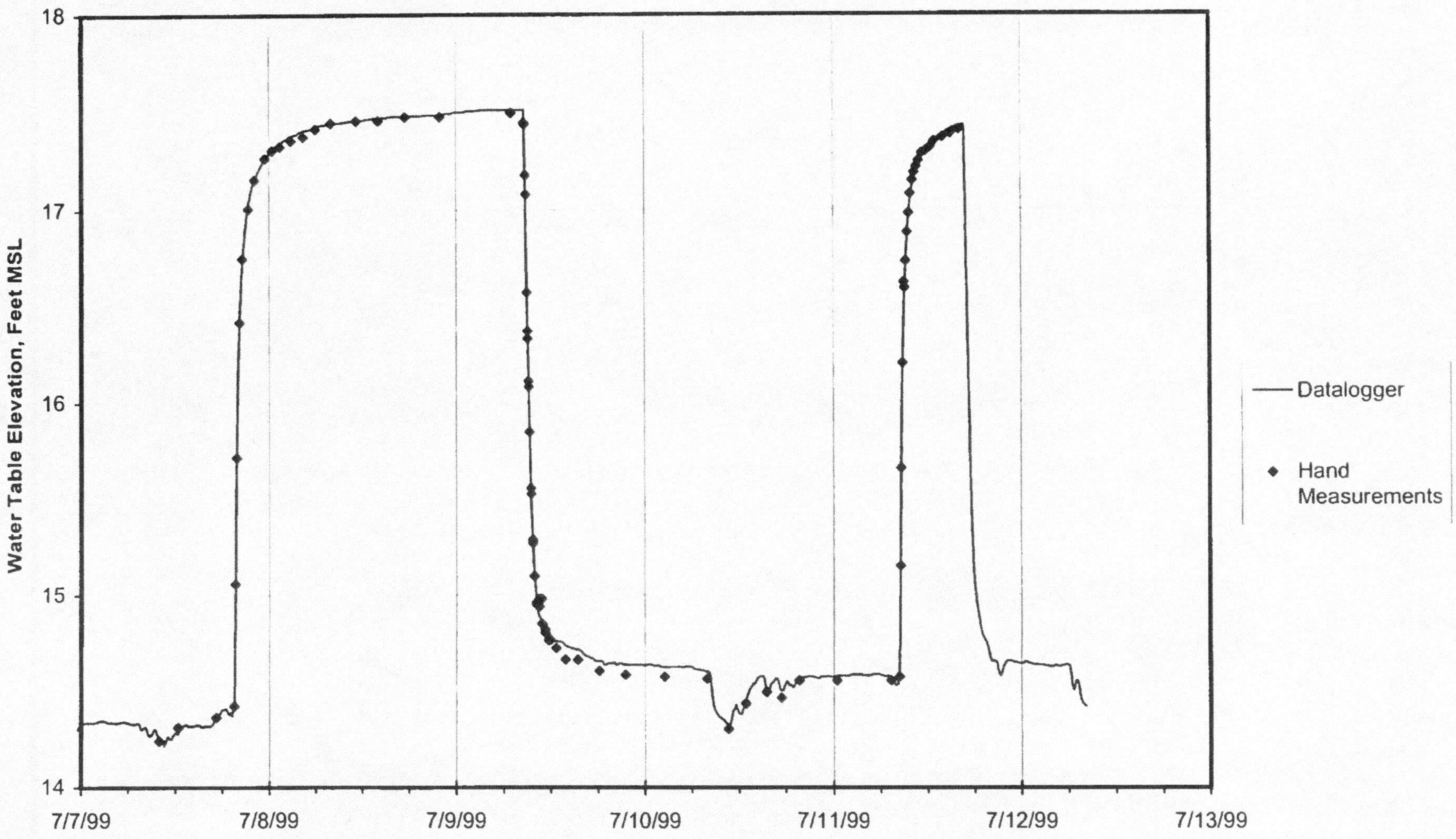

Legend:
— Datalogger
♦ Hand Measurements

X-axis: 7/7/99, 7/8/99, 7/9/99, 7/10/99, 7/11/99, 7/12/99, 7/13/99

Y-axis: Water Table Elevation, Feet MSL (14, 15, 16, 17, 18)

Figure 10. Hydrograph of NPS Monitor Well during the July 1999 aquifer test

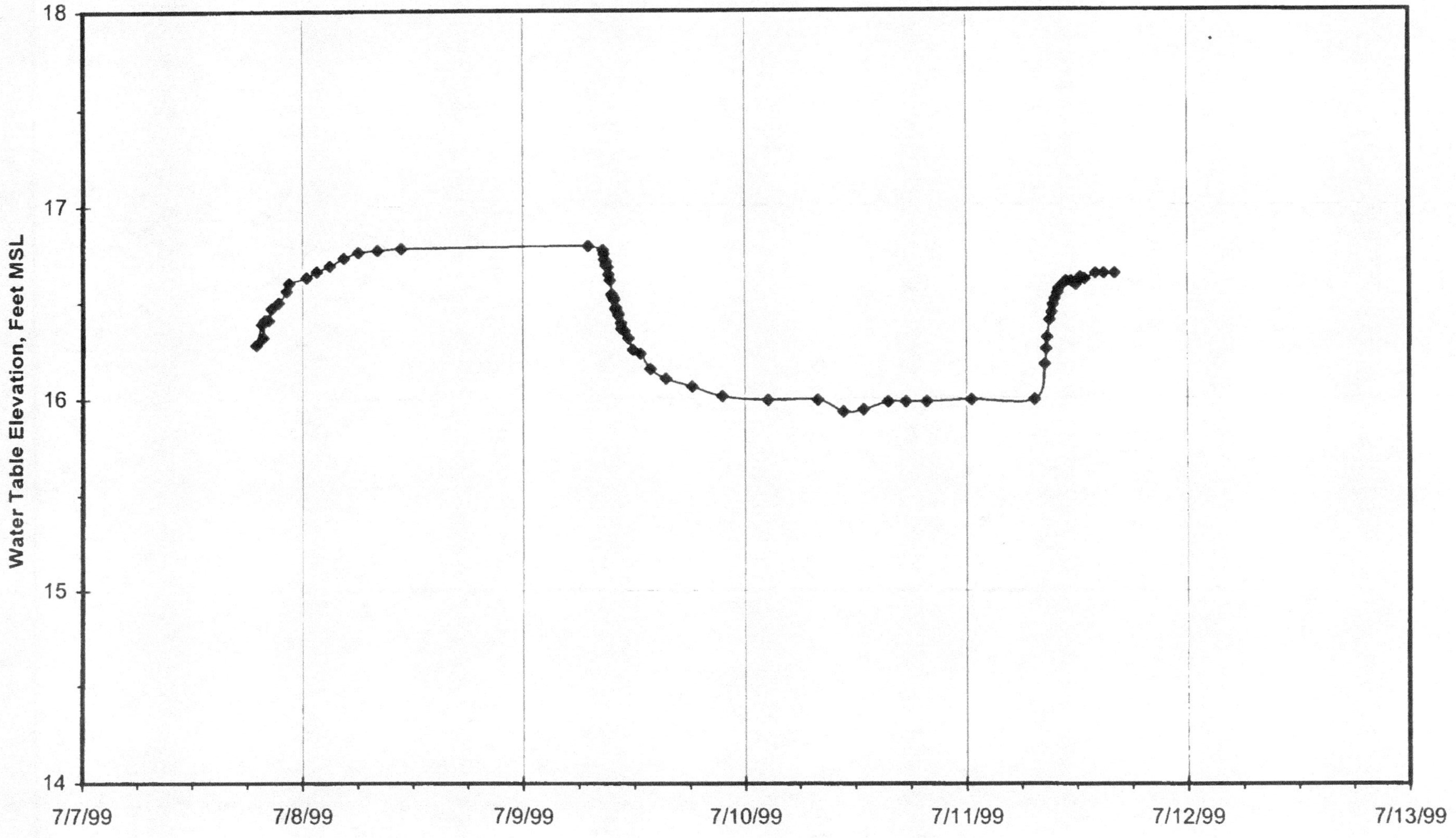

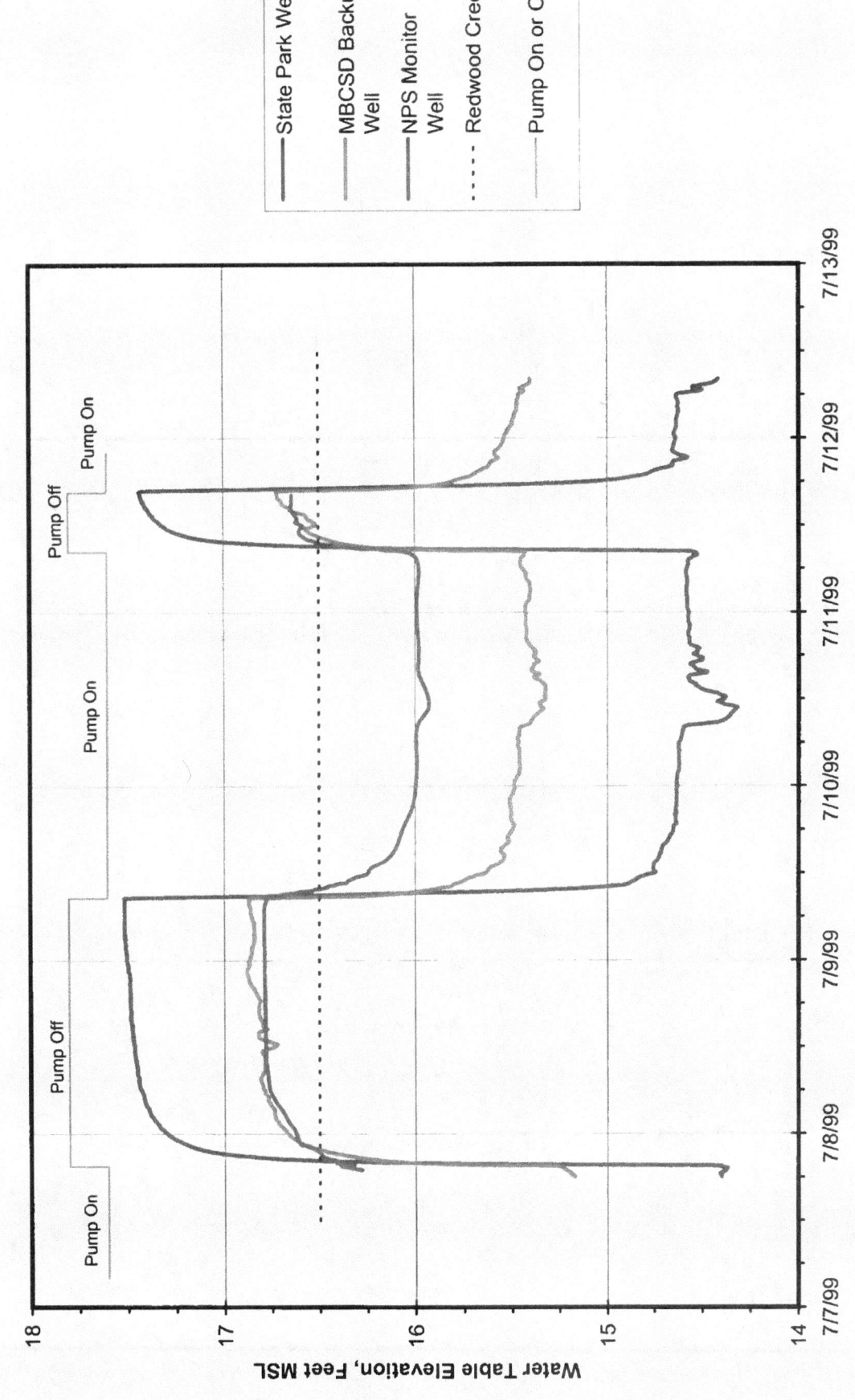

Figure 11. Hydrographs of Deep Monitor Wells during the July 1999 aquifer test

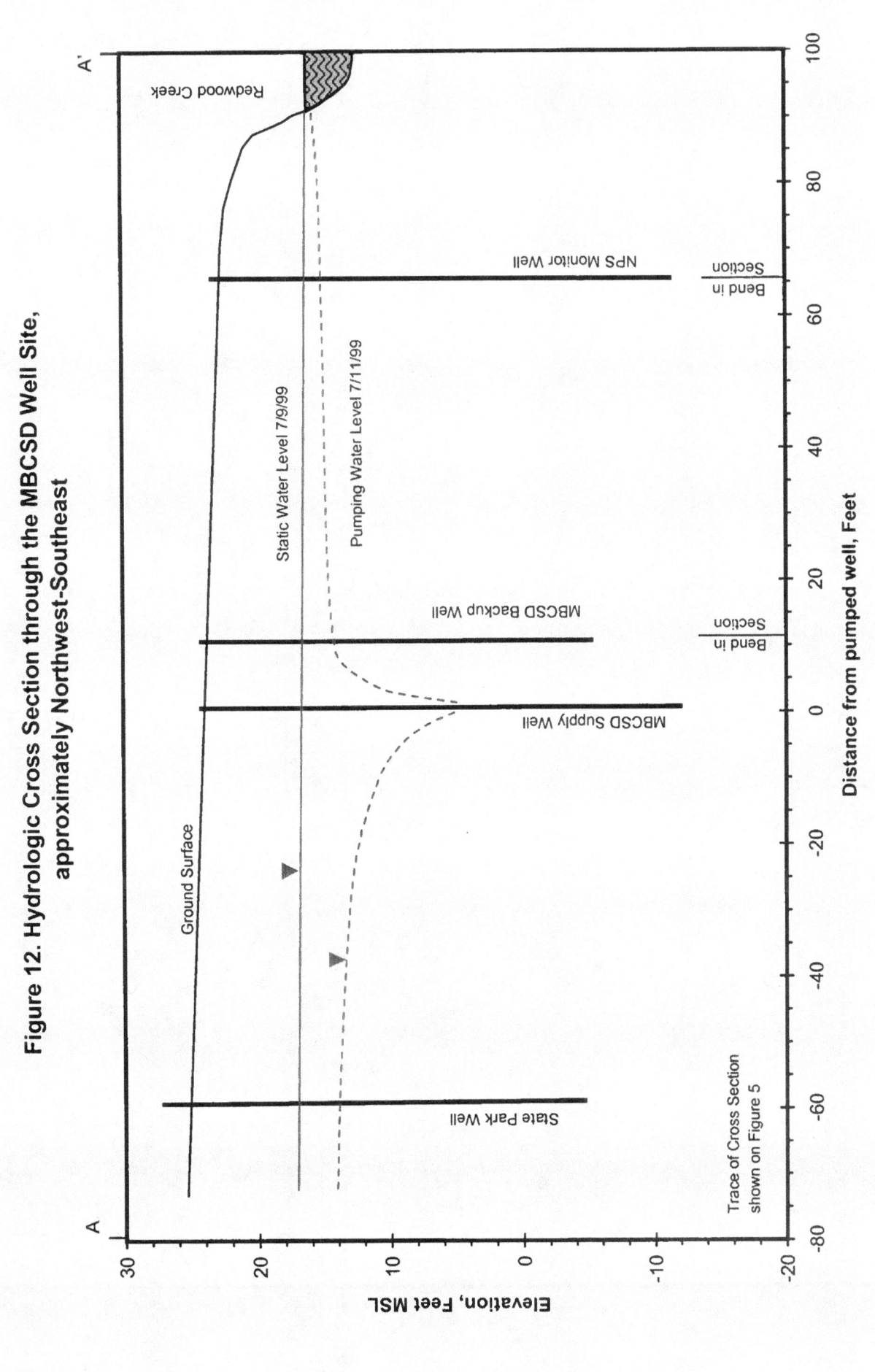

Figure 12. Hydrologic Cross Section through the MBCSD Well Site, approximately Northwest-Southeast

Figure 13. Drawdown at State Park Well matched to Hantush-Jacob Type Curves, Pumping Period 7/9/99 to 7/11/99

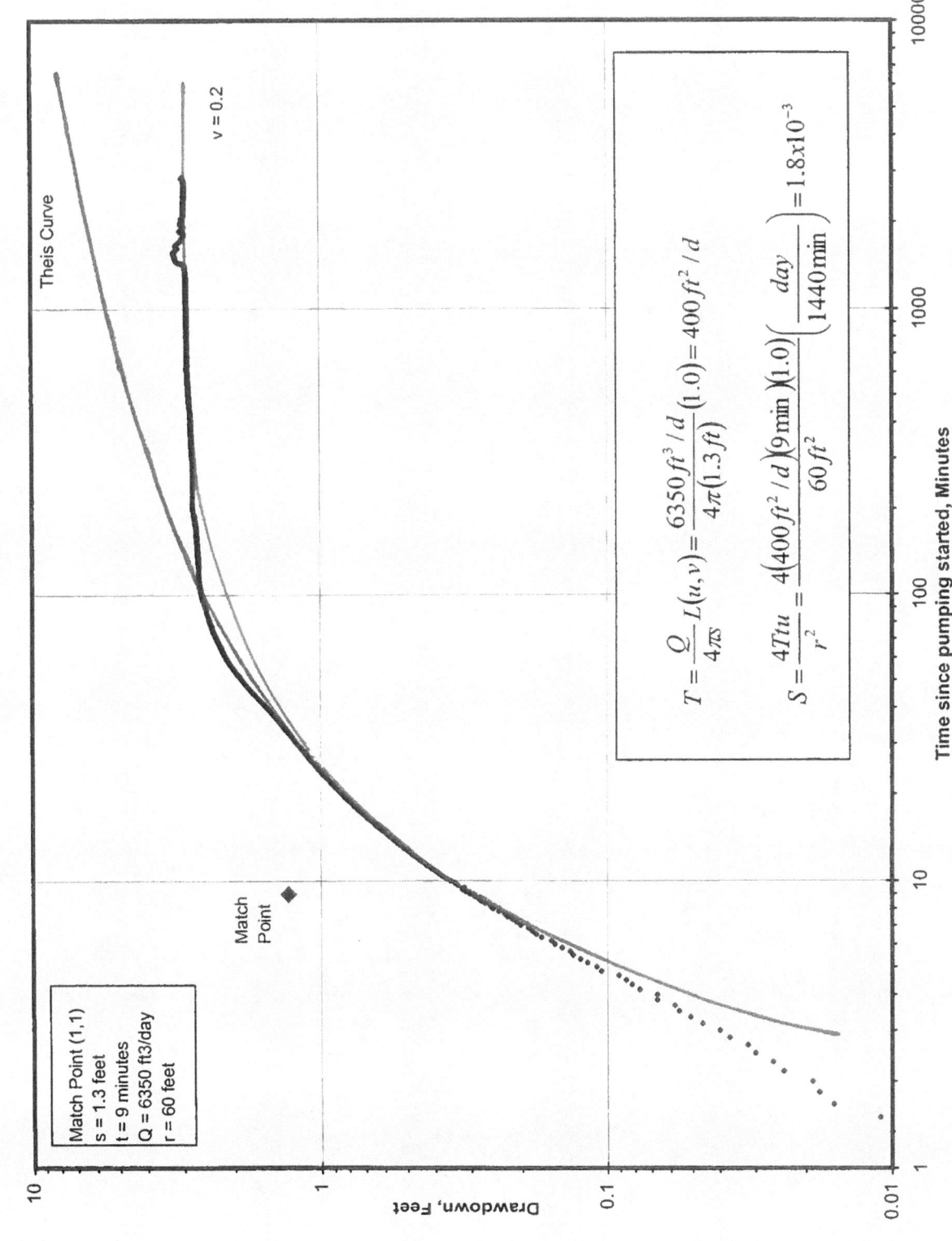

Figure 14. Drawdown at MBCSD Backup Well matched to Hantush-Jacob Type Curves, Pumping Period 7/9/99 to 7/11/99

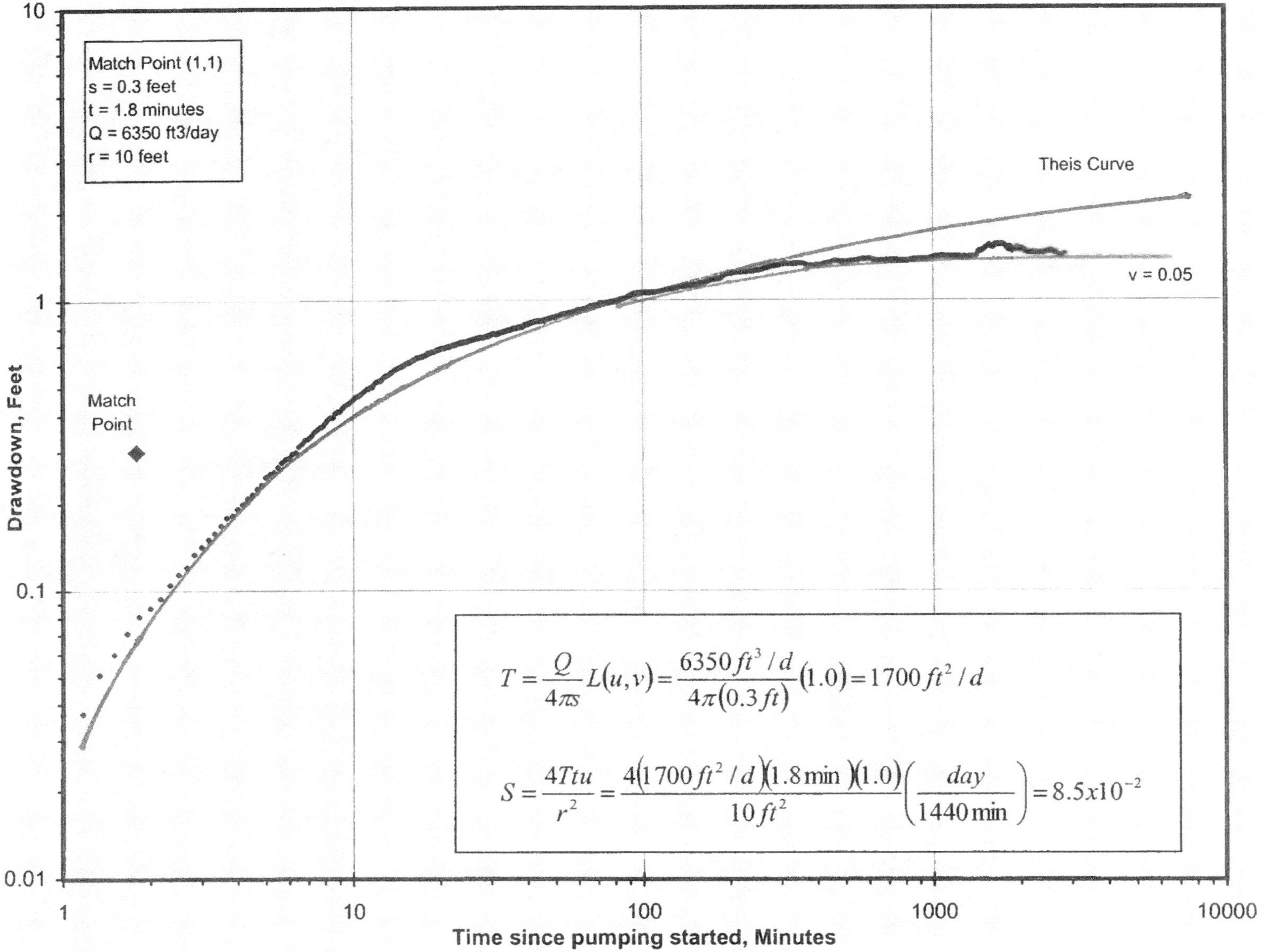

10
1
0.1
0.01
Drawdown, Feet
1
10
100
1000
10000
Time since pumping started, Minutes
Match Point (1,1)
s = 0.3 feet
t = 1.8 minutes
Q = 6350 ft3/day
r = 10 feet
Match Point
Theis Curve
v = 0.05

$$T = \frac{Q}{4\pi s} L(u,v) = \frac{6350\,ft^3/d}{4\pi(0.3\,ft)}(1.0) = 1700\,ft^2/d$$

$$S = \frac{4Ttu}{r^2} = \frac{4(1700\,ft^2/d)(1.8\min)(1.0)}{10\,ft^2}\left(\frac{day}{1440\min}\right) = 8.5x10^{-2}$$

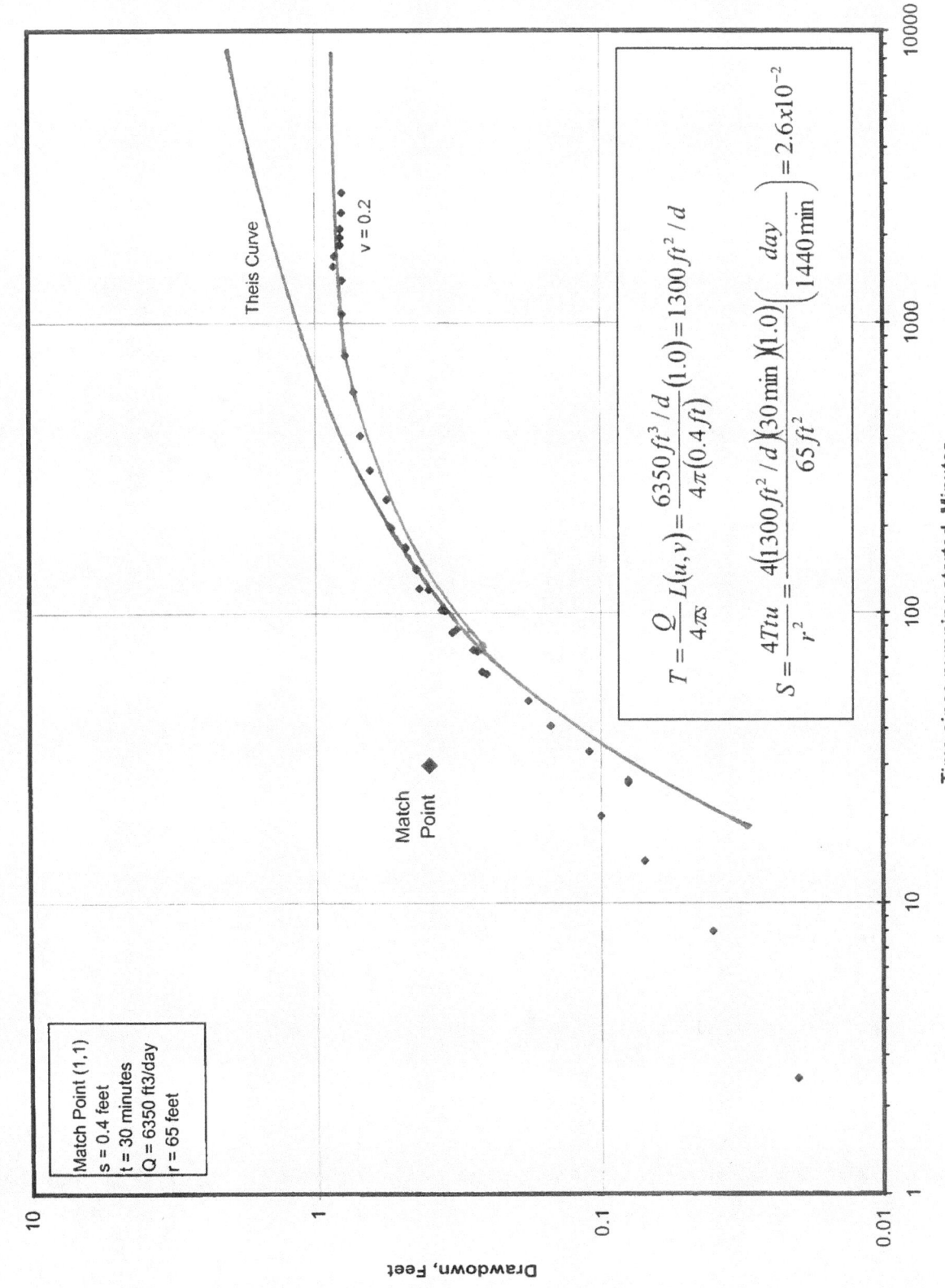

Figure 15. Drawdown at NPS Monitor Well matched to Hantush-Jacob Type Curves, Pumping Period 7/9/99 to 7/11/99

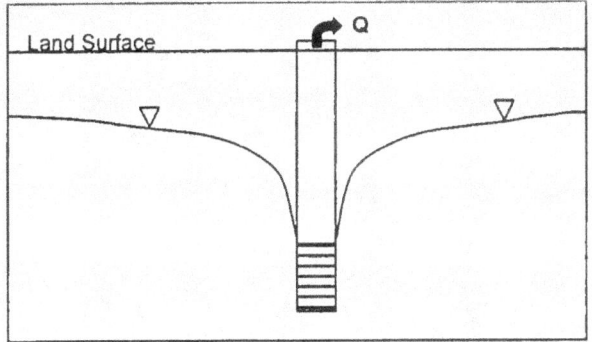

Drawdown in an aquifer with no boundaries

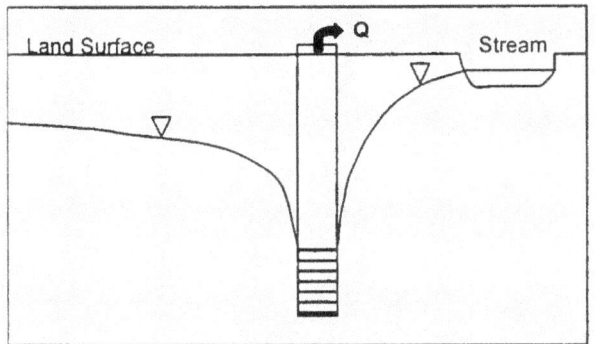

Drawdown in an aquifer bounded by a recharge boundary

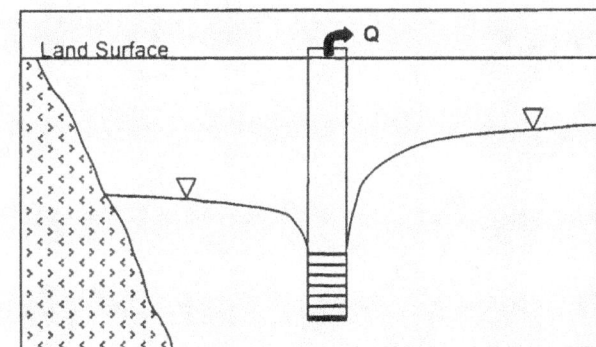

Drawdown in an aquifer bounded by a barrier boundary

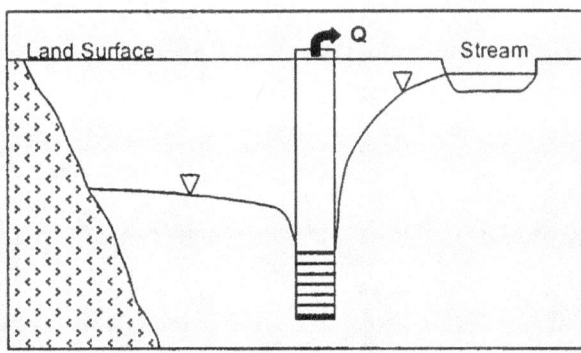

Drawdown in an aquifer bounded by
a recharge and barrier boundary

Figure 16. Hypothesized hydrogeologic cross section

through the MBCSD Well Site

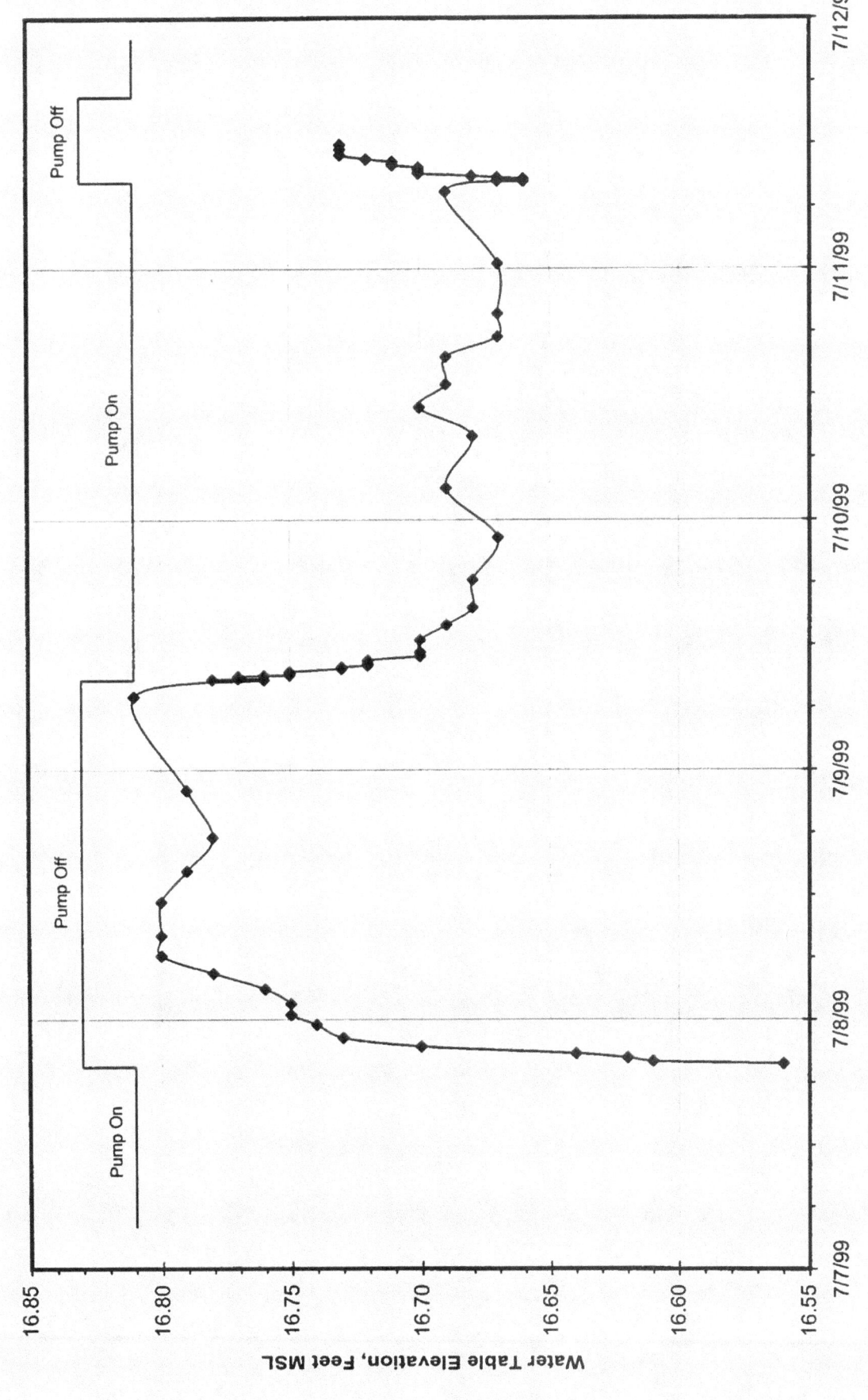

Figure 17. Hydrograph of Piezometer P-2 during the July 1999 aquifer test

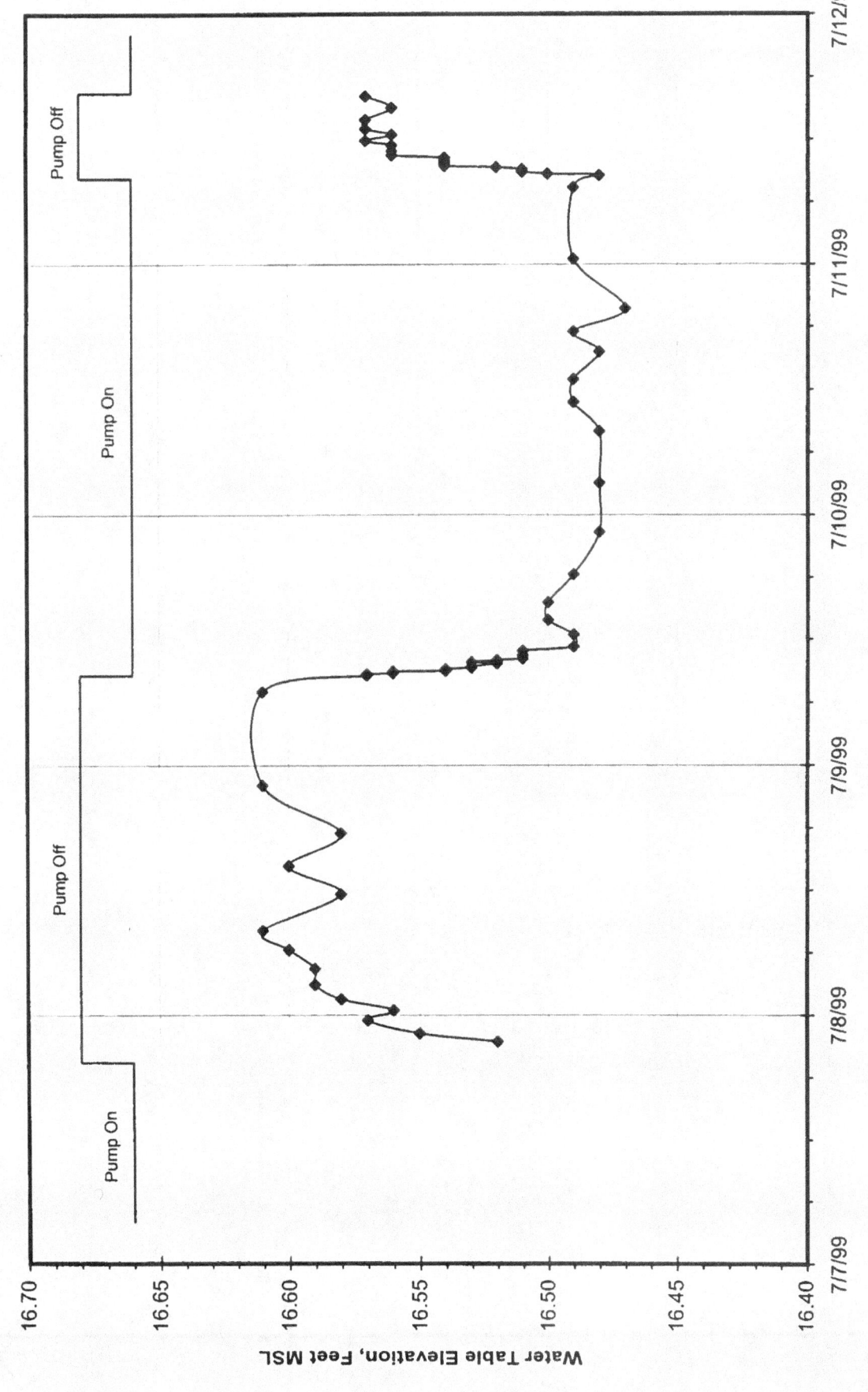

Figure 18. Hydrograph of Piezometer P-9 during the July 1999 aquifer test

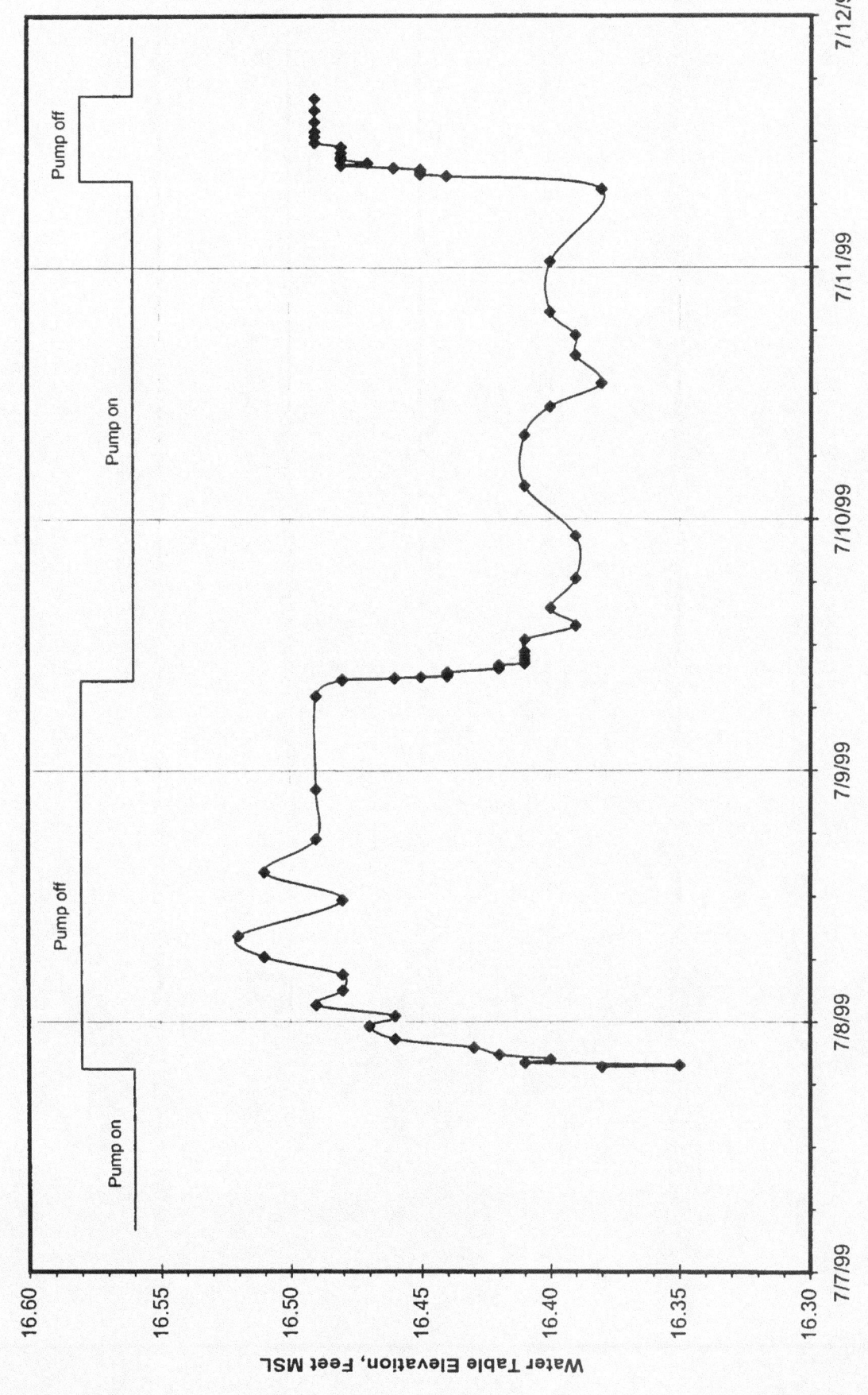

Figure 19. Hydrograph of Piezometer P-6 during the July 1999 aquifer test

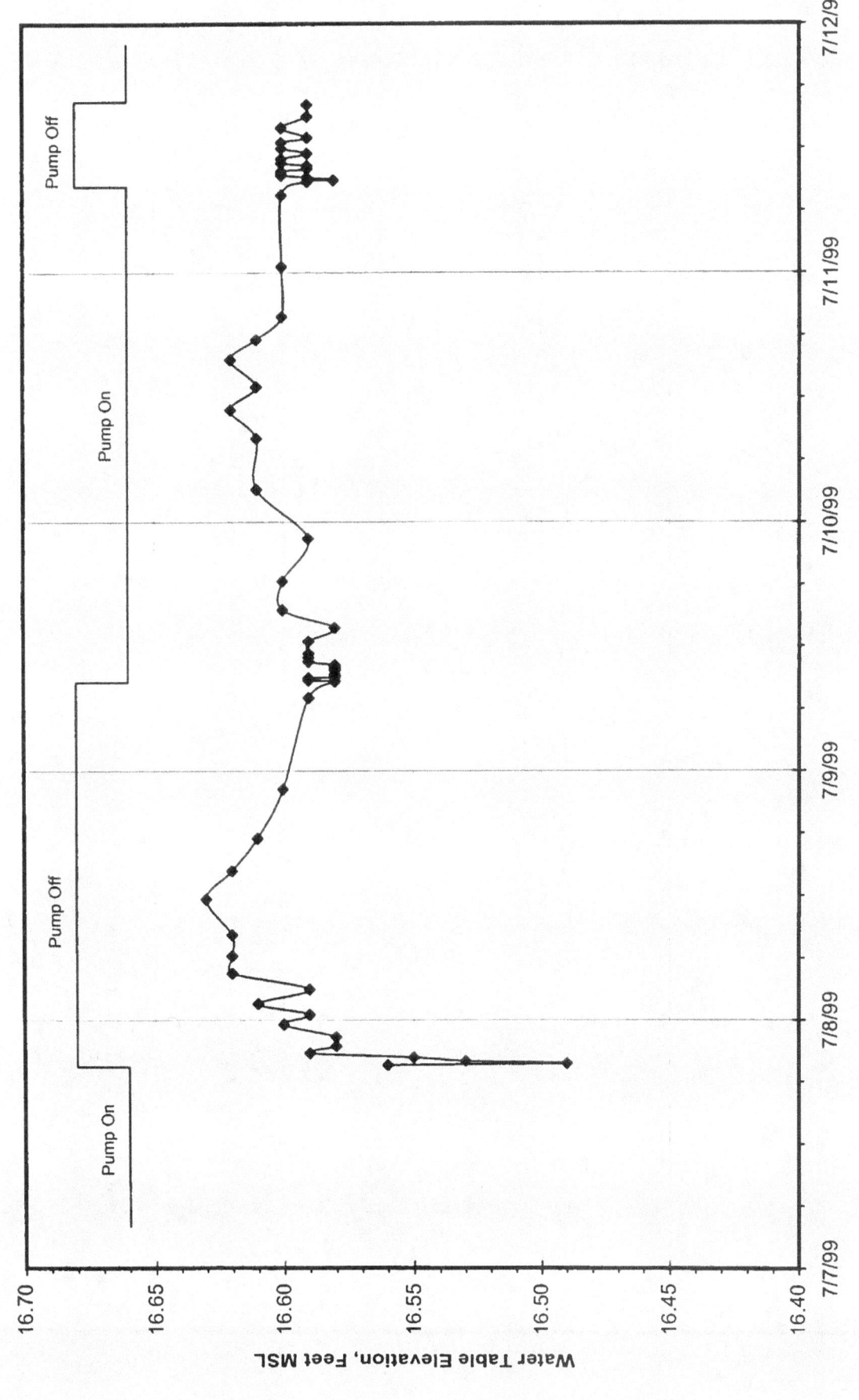

Figure 20. Hydrograph of Piezometer P-10 during the July 1999 aquifer test

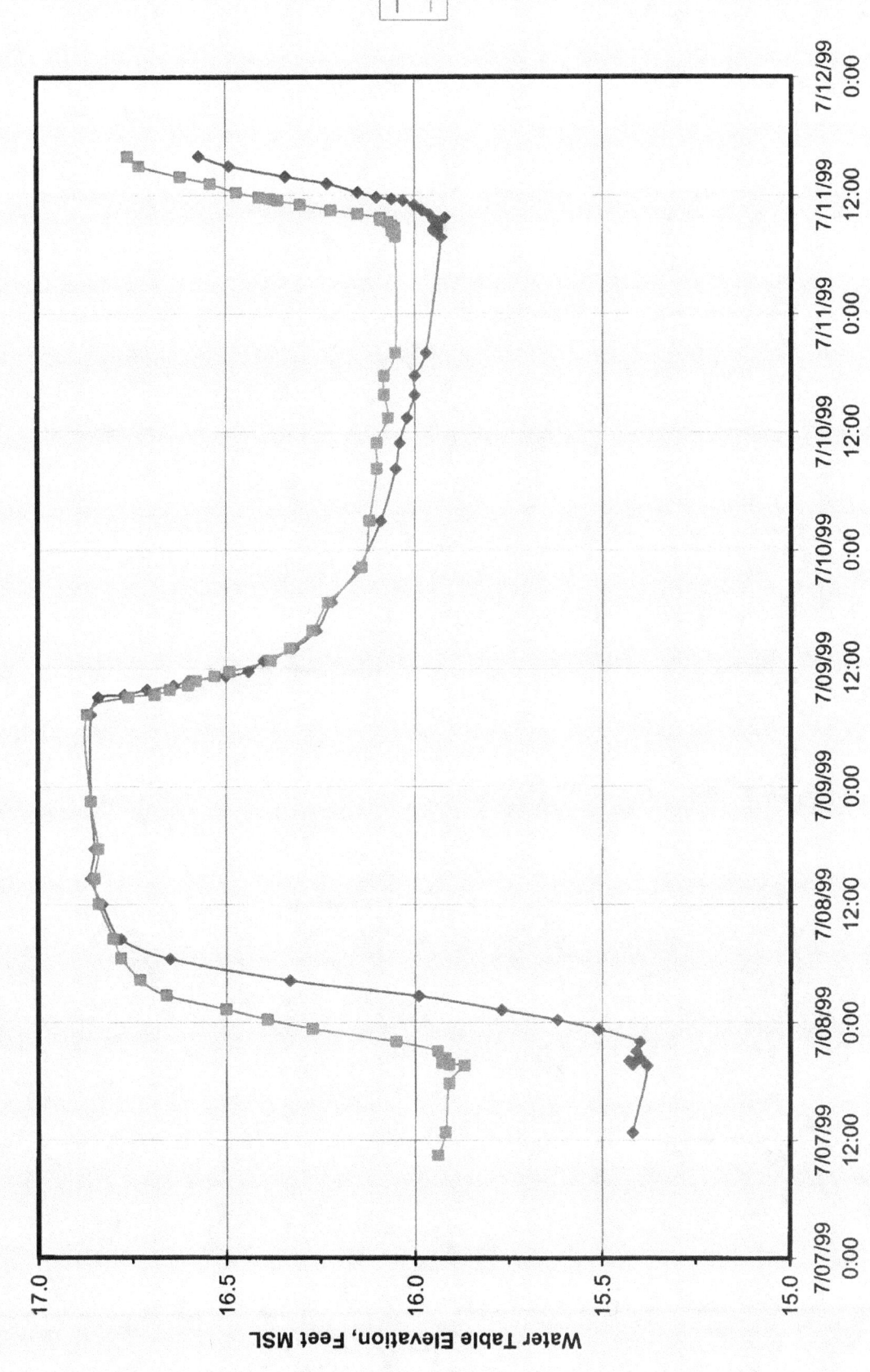

Figure 21. Hydrographs of MBCSD Shallow Monitor Wells, 5-E and 20-E during the July 1999 aquifer test

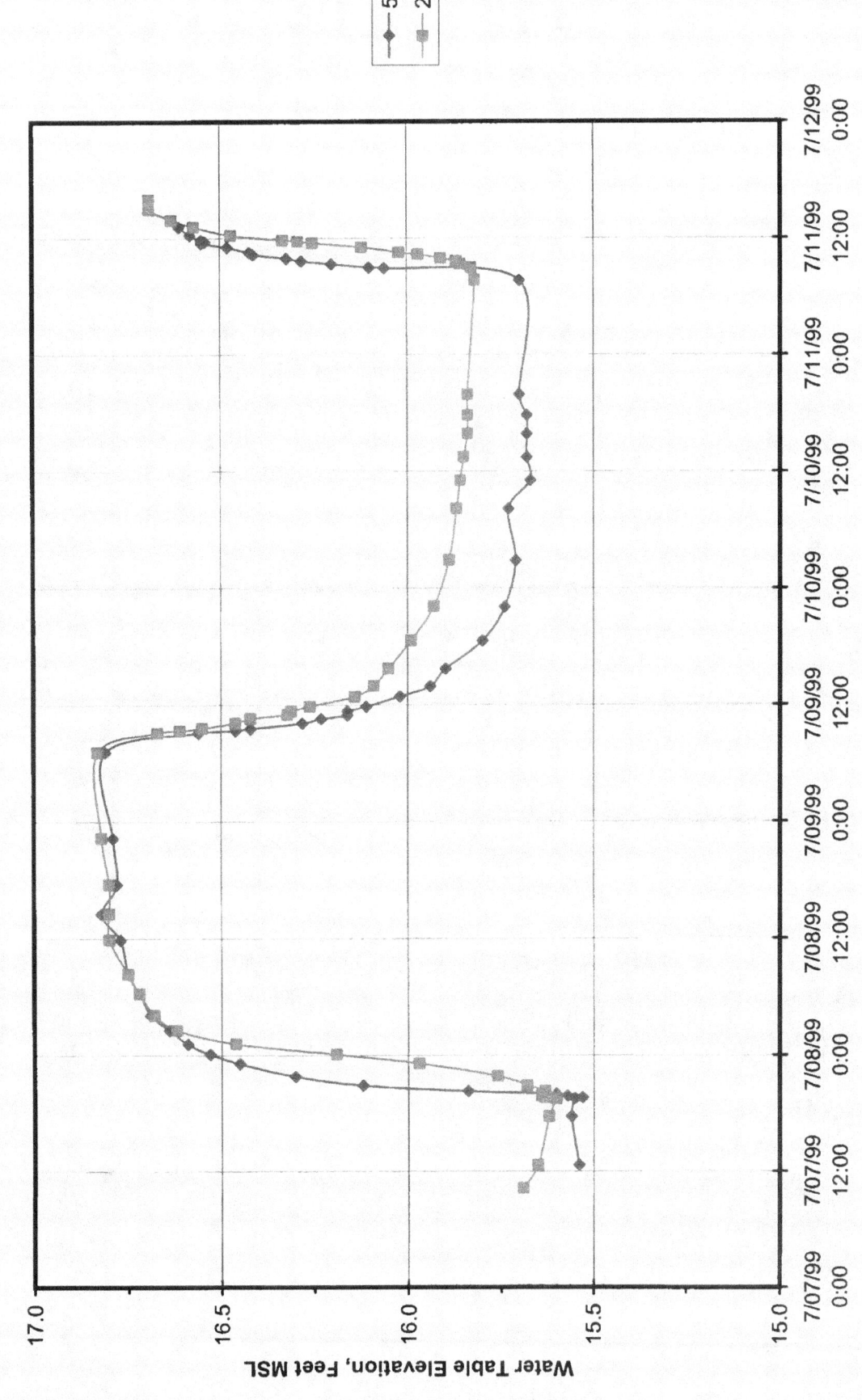

Figure 22. Hydrographs of MBCSD Shallow Monitor Wells, 5-W and 20-W during the July 1999 aquifer test

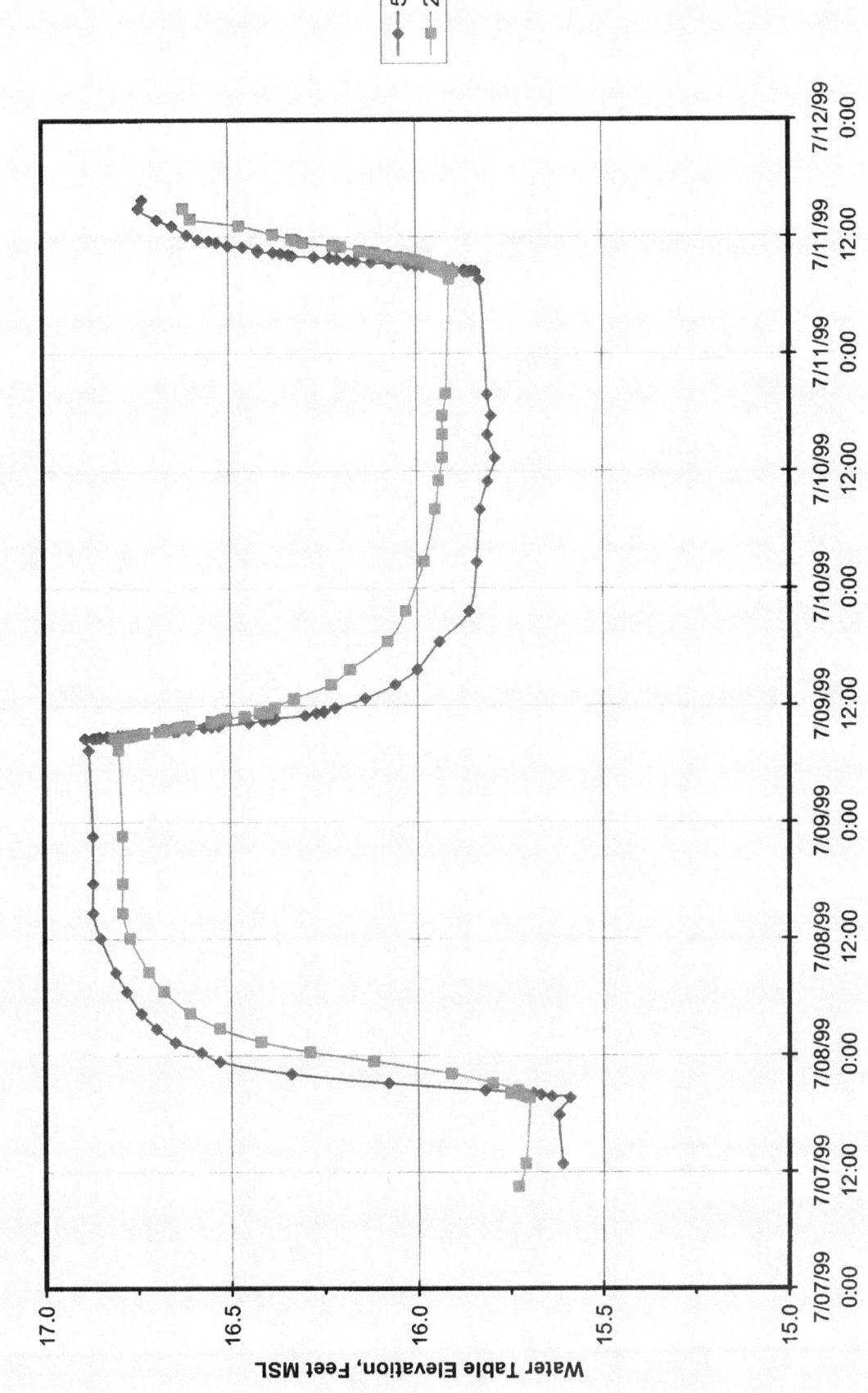

Figure 23. Hydrographs of MBCSD Shallow Monitor Wells, 5-S and 20-S during the July 1999 aquifer test

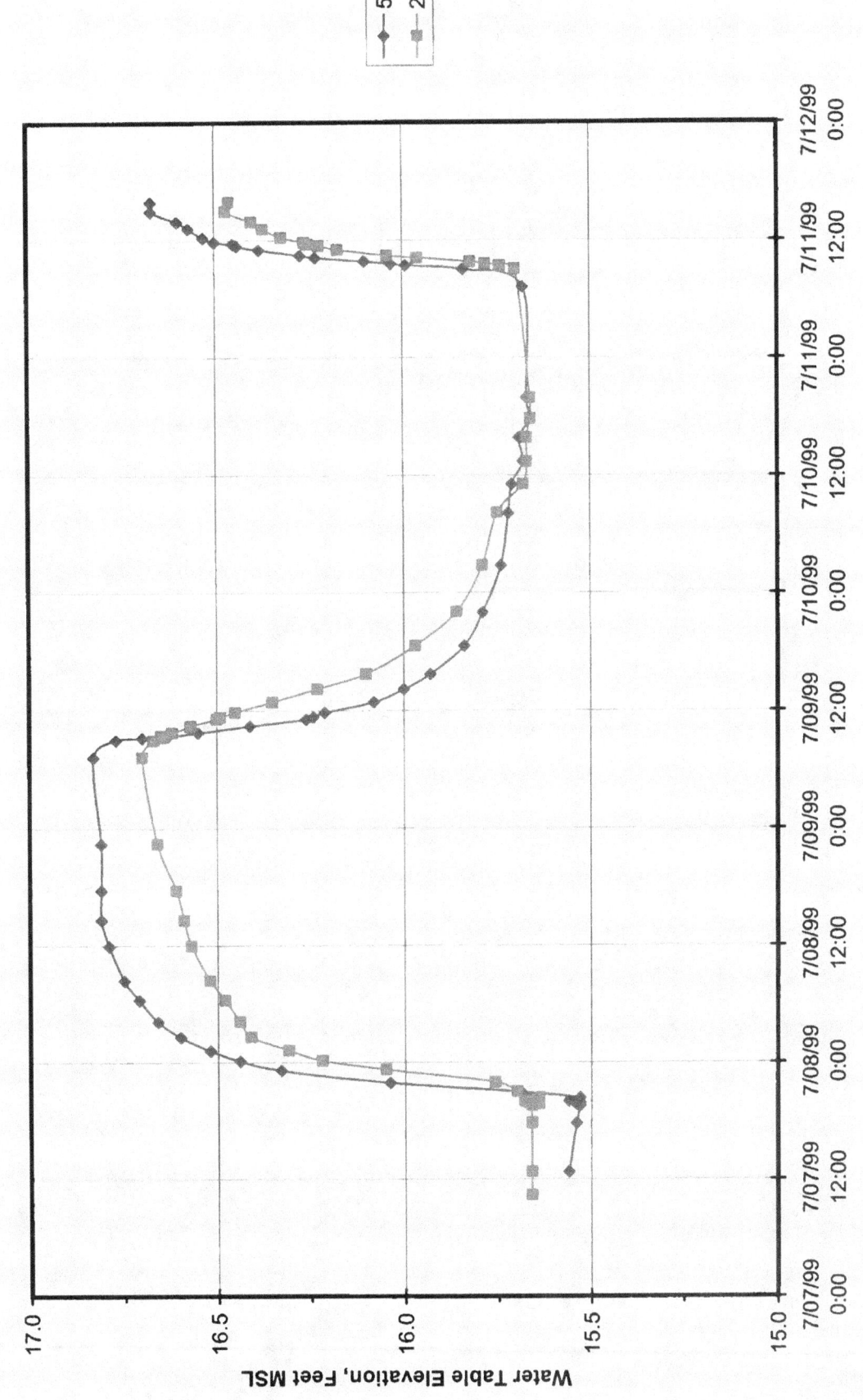

Figure 24. Hydrographs of MBCSD Shallow Monitor Wells, 5-N and 20-N during the July 1999 aquifer test

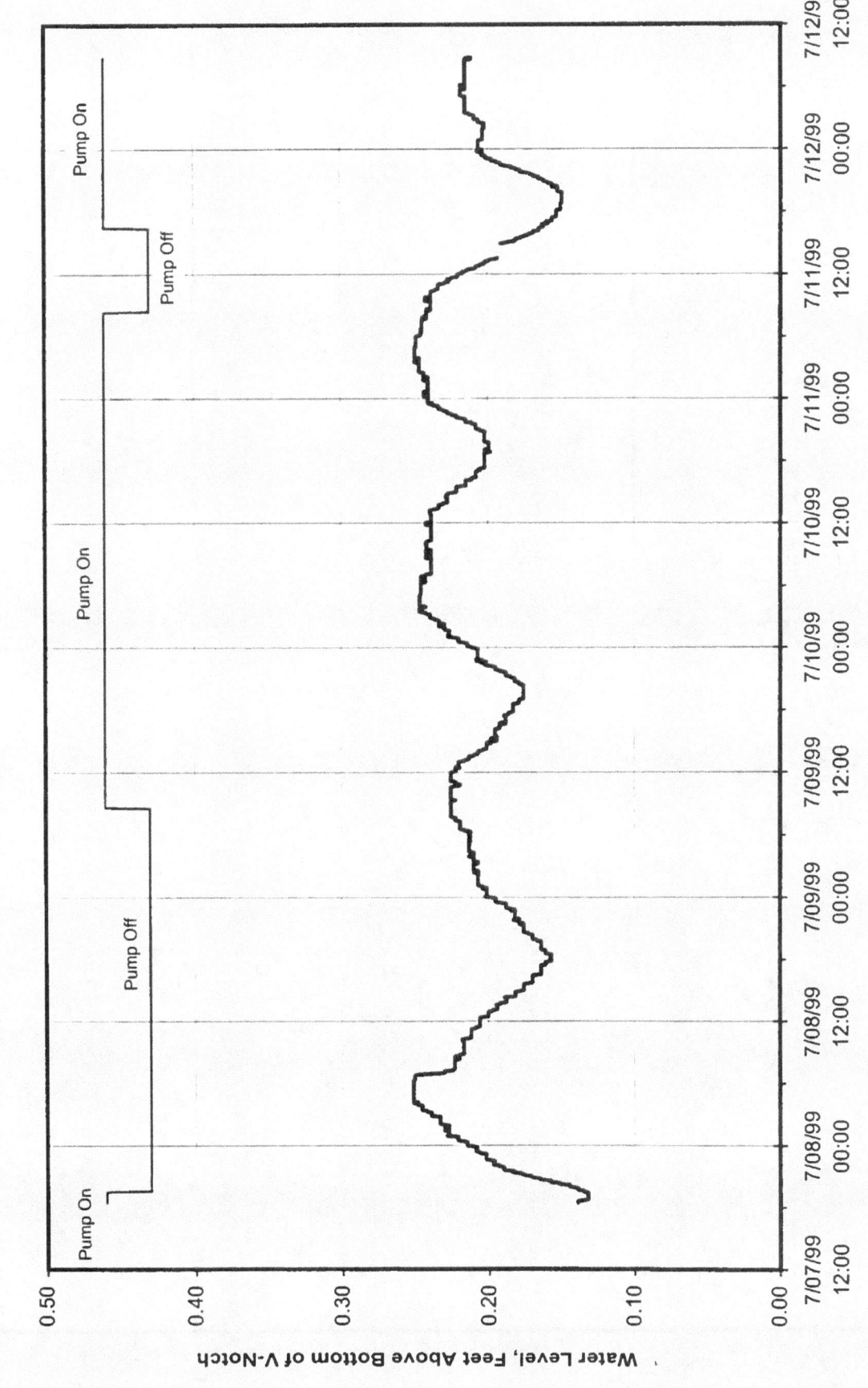

Figure 25. Hydrograph of Upstream Weir during the July 1999 aquifer test (bottom of v-notch = 0.0)

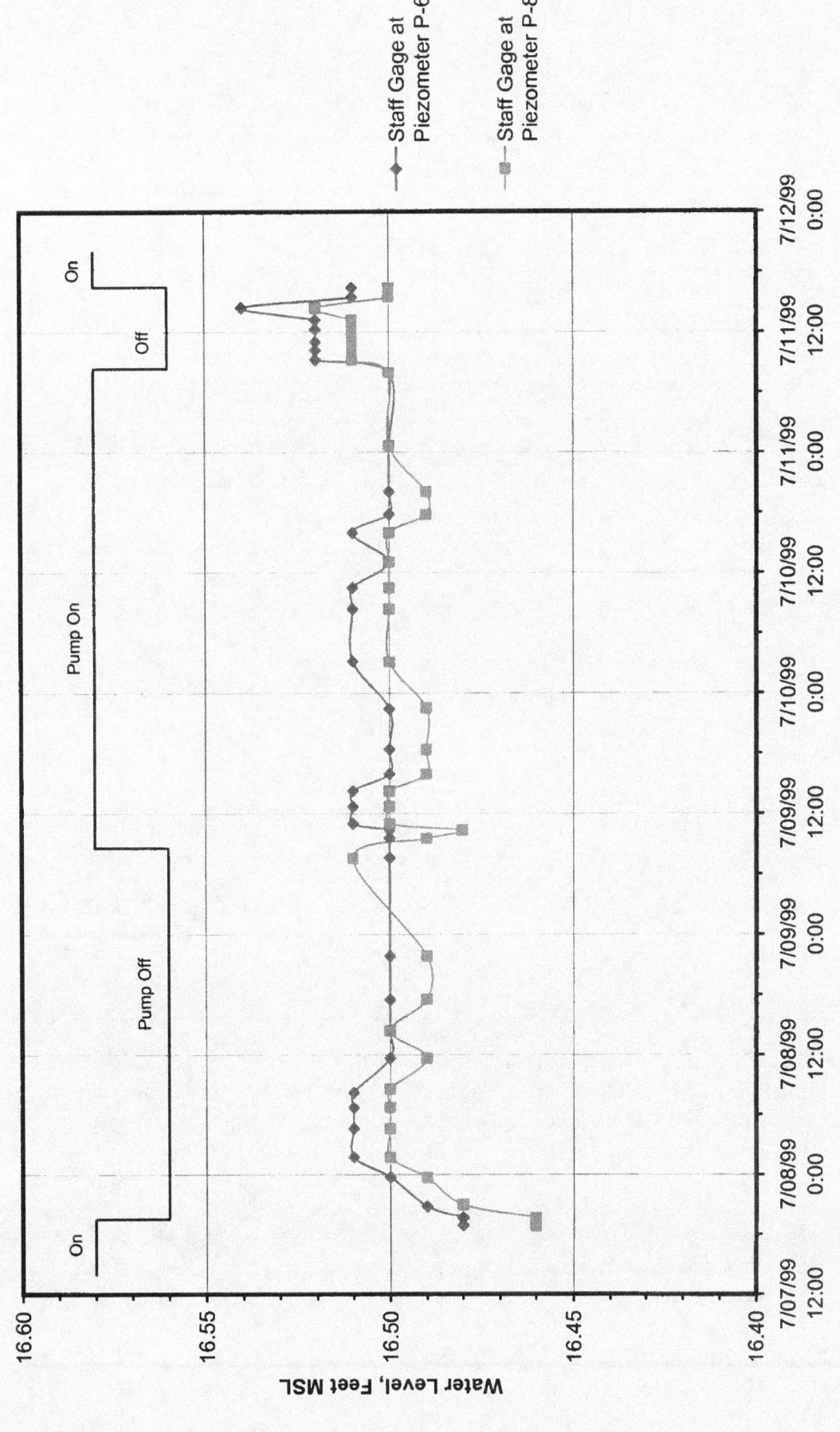

Figure 26. Hydrographs of Staff Gages in Redwood Creek during the July 1999 aquifer test

As the nation's principal conservation agency, the Department of the Interior has the responsibility for most of our nationally owned public lands and natural and cultural resources. This includes fostering wise use of our land and water resources, protecting our fish and wildlife, preserving the environmental and cultural values of our national parks and historical places, and providing for enjoyment of life through outdoor recreation. The Department assesses our energy and mineral resources and works to ensure that their development is in the best interests of all our people. The Department also promotes the goals of the Take Pride in America campaign by encouraging stewardship and citizen responsibility for the public lands and promoting citizen participation in their care. The Department also has a major responsibility for American Indian reservation communities and for people who live in island territories under U.S. administration.

NPS D-397

April 2000